DEE DANCHEV &
ALISTAIR ROSS

RESEARCH ETHICS *for* COUNSELLORS, NURSES *and* SOCIAL WORKERS

Los Angeles | London | New Delhi
Singapore | Washington DC

Los Angeles | London | New Delhi
Singapore | Washington DC

SAGE Publications Ltd
1 Oliver's Yard
55 City Road
London EC1Y 1SP

SAGE Publications Inc.
2455 Teller Road
Thousand Oaks, California 91320

SAGE Publications India Pvt Ltd
B 1/I 1 Mohan Cooperative Industrial Area
Mathura Road
New Delhi 110 044

SAGE Publications Asia-Pacific Pte Ltd
3 Church Street
#10–04 Samsung Hub
Singapore 049483

Editor: Kate Wharton
Editorial assistant: Laura Walmsley
Production editor: Rachel Burrows
Copyeditor: Sarah Bury
Proofreader: Danielle Ray
Marketing manager: Tamara Navaratnam
Cover design: Jennifer Crisp
Typeset by: C&M Digitals (P) Ltd, Chennai, India
Printed in Great Britain by Henry Ling Limited, at
the Dorset Press, Dorchester, DT1 1HD

MIX
Paper from
responsible sources
FSC® C013985

© Dee Danchev and Alistair Ross 2014

First published 2014

Library of Congress Control Number: 2013935446

British Library Cataloguing in Publication data

A catalogue record for this book is available from
the British Library

ISBN 978-1-4462-5335-9
ISBN 978-1-4462-5336-6 (pbk)

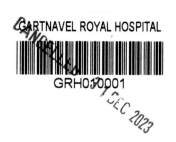

...ETHICS *for*

..., NURSES

...WORKERS

For Alex and Judy

Contents

About the authors

Dee Danchev is a Chartered Psychologist. After an earlier career in medical social work she focused on developing her therapeutic skills and trained as a counsellor. She is primarily a practitioner and has worked in a variety of educational, medical and emergency service settings. This has included managing a university counselling, health and disability service, and the post of supervisor for the Metropolitan Police Service counsellors. She has had a parallel career as a tutor and lecturer on social work, counselling and counselling psychology training courses at Keele University and City University, London. She has supervised postgraduate research since 1992 and until recently was research tutor for students on the Masters course in Psychodynamic Practice at Oxford University. Dee is currently Pastoral Advisor at Nuffield College, Oxford, where she provides counselling and psychological support for the students, fellows and staff. She is an enthusiastic supporter of the British Psychological Society's Qualification in Counselling Psychology, which provides an independent route to becoming a counselling psychologist. She currently serves as Chair of the Board of Assessors for this qualification.

Her recent publications include a chapter on counselling in education for the third edition of the *Handbook of Counselling Psychology* (SAGE, 2010) and the practitioner's perspective for the chapter on depression for *Common Presenting Issues for Psychotherapeutic Practice* (SAGE, 2014).

Alistair Ross initially trained as a Baptist Minister and worked in South London, Kent and Birmingham. He subsequently did an experiential therapeutic training course at Claybury Psychiatric Hospital in Essex and worked as a pastoral counsellor and practical theologian. He is a senior accredited psychodynamic counsellor and supervisor, as well as a dynamic interpersonal therapist. Alistair is Director of Psychodynamic Studies and University Lecturer in Psychotherapy at Oxford University. He is also Dean and Fellow of Kellogg College.

Alistair enjoys being Chair of the British Association for Counselling and Psychotherapy's Professional Ethics and Quality Standards Committee, which makes ethics a continually live experience. He is a member of the editorial board for *Practical Theology* and reviews editor for *The European Journal of Psychotherapy and Counselling*.

Alistair's research is on the emergence of spirituality in contemporary psychoanalysis, which he has termed 'sacred psychoanalysis'. Publications include *Counselling Skills for Church and Faith Community Workers* (Open University Press, 2003) and 'Psychodynamic counselling, religion and spirituality', in S. Wheeler (ed.), *Difference and Diversity in Counselling: Contemporary Psychodynamic Practice* (Palgrave Macmillan, 2006). Alistair has authored and co-authored a wide range of articles, including such diverse but intriguing subjects as: 'Theology and terrorism: Interview and analysis'; 'Grotstein's "Black Hole" and working with Borderline Personality'; 'A new pluralism: A paradigm of pluralisms'; 'Inside the experience of anorexia nervosa: A narrative thematic analysis'; 'The writings of Peter Lomas'; and 'The relational: A postmodern meta-narrative'.

To relax, Alistair enjoys hill-walking and scrambling in Scotland, the land of his birth.

Acknowledgements

Dee – I would like to thank Paul Gordon, who encouraged me to write. I would also like to thank my formative social work and counselling teachers Tony Bolger and Val Harding Davies. I have a special debt of gratitude to John McLeod, who provided me with an invaluable education in research theory and practice.

Alistair – I would like to thank my colleagues at the British Association for Counselling and Psychotherapy, especially Tim Bond, Nancy Rowlands, Helen Coles, Hadyn Williams and Sarah Millward as well as the Professional Ethics and Quality Standards Committee.

We would both like to thank Alice Oven, Kate Wharton, Laura Walmsley and Rachel Burrows at Sage for their helpful advice and encouragement.

We are indebted to the following people for stimulating and sustaining conversations: Sarah Bartlett, Nic Bayley, Chris Chambers, Jemma Chambers, Geoff Colmer, Mike Ellis, Barbara Fayers, Paul and Gill Goodliff, Hannah Gormley, Jack Gormley, Sarah Grochala, Pam Horrocks, Oliver Horrocks, Diane Miller, Stephen Pattison, Toby Ross, Adelheid Scholten, Dee Stanfield, Paul Stoop, and Ray Woolf.

We would like to thank the Warden, fellows, students and staff of Nuffield College, Oxford; the President, fellows, students and staff of Kellogg College, Oxford; and the Department of Continuing Education at Oxford University. They all provide us with enriching work environments. Thanks are also due to the students of the M.St. programme in Psychodynamic Practice. They have contributed to our understanding of research ethics with lively and thoughtful discussions about their ethical dilemmas.

Especial thanks for permission to reproduce their work to Jemma C. Chambers, Christian Jarrett, Elana Newman, Traci Willard, Robert Sinclair, Danny Kaloupek, Petroc Sumner, Frederic Boy, and Chris Chambers. We would also like to thank the British Psychological Society and The Guardian newspaper for permission to reproduce work that was initially published on their websites.

Finally, heartfelt thanks to our partners Alex Danchev and Judy Ross for their encouragement and unfailing support throughout this project.

Introduction

Mention research ethics to novice researchers and you will find a common pattern of response. It is a mixture of indignation, trepidation and irritation. The indignation comes from a conviction that 'of course I will behave ethically, I don't need to be told this'. The trepidation arises from an anxiety that 'I will get something wrong, I will be complained about, shamed and at worst be asked to appear before an ethical committee'. The irritation stems from the fact that it is necessary at the beginning of the process to produce a research proposal and apply to an ethical committee for approval. The ethical approval forms often appear to be lengthy, opaque and intimidating, and it seems as if the whole project and all the dilemmas that may be encountered have to be thought through in detail before the research has scarcely begun.

We are not primarily researchers or philosophers but practitioners striving to do the best we can in an imperfect world and we are approaching research ethics from this perspective. We both have enduring interests in the philosophy, psychology and social science that contributes to the understanding of human relationships. Focusing on the ethical basis of research reminds us that ethical thinking is an intrinsic part of who we are and how we relate to others. Kant's dictum sums up the overriding challenge that faces us: 'Act in such a way that you treat humanity, whether in your own person or in the person of an other, always at the same time as an end and never simply as a means [to an end]' (Kant, 1993 [1785]: 36). We are especially influenced by the work of Emmanuel Levinas, whose philosophy is pivotal in deepening our understanding of our responsibilities towards others, and the linkages between the personal, social and political worlds.

Our aim for this book is to provide a guide to ethical research practice that will enable researchers to widen their ethical thinking and negotiate the ethical decisions that they will need to make while carrying out their research projects. We are aware that researchers would like a book that provided clear-cut answers for their ethical dilemmas and decisions, but it is not possible to provide one as ethical problems are rarely simple. Our view is that expanding researchers' understanding of the history of research ethics and increasing their familiarity with the complexities of ethical theory and practice raises their confidence. It is then possible for them to make their own decisions and view ethical research practice as creative and enabling. The research pathway is rarely straightforward, but working through the challenges that it presents to achieve the best possible ethical solutions can be very rewarding.

We hope that this book will prove useful for a wide range of professionals, including counsellors, psychotherapists, mental health workers, social workers, nurses, and practitioners working within the voluntary sector. Increasing numbers of people from the caring professions are undertaking postgraduate research degrees and are engaging in research projects within their workplaces to establish a firm evidence and knowledge base for practice.

Research is often divided by whether the methodology used is quantitative or qualitative. When considering research from an ethical perspective, a more relevant way of looking at it is what is the degree of contact with participants and relevant others, and how much intrusion into their lives does the research involve? Qualitative researchers tend to have mainly face-to-face contact with participants but sometimes use distance methods, such as asking people to send them written texts. However, quantitative researchers may use methods that involve them meeting their participants and their research can also include delving deeply into people's lives or conducting research that involves some form of experiment or physical intervention. Both qualitative and quantitative researchers alike need to maintain ethical awareness and so we hope that researchers using a variety of methodologies will find this book useful.

Gaining ethical approval for projects is an essential part of the research process and can seem to be a daunting hurdle to new researchers. Researchers often long for a simple list of necessary actions which, if fulfilled, will enable them to gain the necessary permissions. Ethical research guidelines aim to do this and are useful, but researchers soon realise that the guidelines are not universally applicable and that unanticipated problems can occur throughout the research process. In fact, as we proceed with our projects, it becomes clear that the entire research process is freighted with ethical decisions. We certainly do not have all the answers but we hope that this book will give practitioners the knowledge and skills to enable them to be ethically mindful throughout their research projects and to have the confidence to make ethical decisions that are appropriate for the particular circumstances of their study.

This book is designed to take the reader through the steps and theoretical understanding that we believe are necessary to conduct ethics-based research. It follows an ethical research cycle. We have devised this cycle to show how the elements of ethics-based research link up. Ethical philosophies and theories continually evolve over time and are shaped according to philosophical, cultural, political and religious beliefs. Each social context generates its own ethical theories; and ethical research codes and frameworks are derived from these theories. The codes and frameworks guide researchers but the researcher has also to develop their own ethical capacity in order to behave ethically. A fundamental facet of this capacity is a heightened awareness of their responsibilities towards research participants and any others who may be affected by the research; and this includes the ability to form and sustain ethical relationships. The participants and others need to be held in mind throughout the process of ethically obtaining and analysing data. Ethical considerations are a central aspect of the next stage of the cycle, which is the dissemination of research findings to the wider community. Disseminated knowledge obtained through research in turn can impact on the ethical conduct and development of social contexts and this completes the cycle.

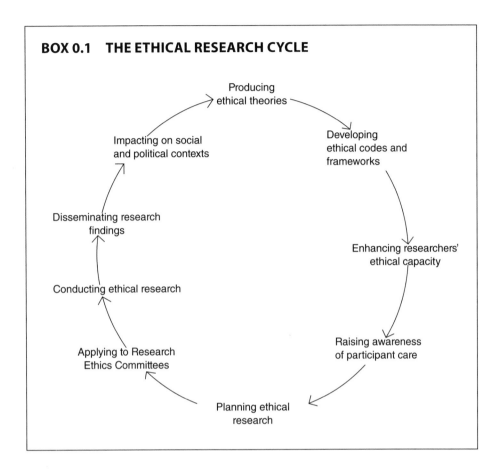

BOX 0.1   THE ETHICAL RESEARCH CYCLE

We begin this book by thinking about the personal development and reflection that researchers need to engage in before embarking on projects. It then focuses on the care of participants and the researcher–participant relationship. A guide to dealing with ethical dilemmas and making decisions when planning a research project follows and a section on making applications to ethical committees is included. Finally, we consider the wider social and political ethical implications of research and its dissemination.

Chapter 1 underlines the importance of adopting an ethical stance in relation to research. Ethical thinking, it is argued, needs to be applied and foregrounded throughout the research process. Research ethics currently tend to be based on the ethical principles of beneficence (do good), non-maleficence (do no harm), autonomy, justice, fidelity and veracity. While principle ethics can provide a useful guide for solving dilemmas, as will be explored in Chapter 5, we argue for a deeper level of ethical thinking that goes beyond the adherence to rules and regulations. We consider the usefulness of research ethics guidelines and argue that ethical thinking needs to be embedded in the person of the researcher for ethical practice to occur. To achieve this we consider and critique the usefulness of virtue ethics and explore the desirable virtues that may constitute the ethical researcher. We underline the ethical importance of decentring from the researcher's own worldview and establishing a reflexive approach to their research. We also explore the means by which researchers can extend their ability to be reflexive. In a further section we consider researchers' responsibilities towards themselves, and highlight the importance of researcher safety while conducting research. We also encourage self-reflection about their choice of research subject as researchers may have consciously or unconsciously chosen a subject that has painful emotional connections. In the final section of Chapter 1 we emphasise the need for researchers to maintain their self-care and discuss the issues related to researcher guilt and shame, and the secondary traumatisation of researchers who are exploring the impact of traumatic experiences on their participants.

Chapter 2 focuses on the research participant and reviews how the status of the participant has moved from the objectified position of research subject to participant and to co-researcher. We consider the meaning of these participant positions for both the participant and the researcher, and how this positioning impacts on the approach of the researcher. We then review the history of research that has led to a greater focus on participant care. This is followed by an exploration of the philosophy of Emmanuel Levinas and we use his thinking to discuss the level of responsibility that researchers have towards their participants. Our focus on the care of the participant also includes a consideration of participant vulnerability. We explore the issues involved in conducting research with children and the range of adult participants who may be described as vulnerable. Our overall aim for this chapter is to assist researchers in sensitising themselves to their responsibilities towards their participants and gaining an understanding of what it may mean to be a participant in their research project.

Chapter 3 considers the relationship between the researcher and their participants. The origins of relational ethics are described and their relevance to the researcher–participant relationship is highlighted. The context of the research and the researcher's choice of subject both impact on the establishment of the research relationship and the ethical implications of these factors are explored. Practitioners are skilled at building relationships with clients and several issues arise in relation to these skills. Do these relational abilities create difficulties for the researcher and for the participant or do they enhance the process? How does the research relationship differ from a therapeutic relationship? This subject area is particularly important for therapeutic practitioners as their unique skills can be used, consciously or unconsciously, to both ethical and unethical ends in their engagement with participants. The dynamics of the research relationship are explored and we highlight the pitfalls and positive aspects. Finally, we explore the ending of the research relationship and consider the ethics of transitional and continuing relationships.

Chapter 4 considers the all-important issue of trust and how it can be established and maintained during the research process. We consider the ethics of trust and explain how knowledge of this area can underpin the practical actions that are necessary to establish a trusting relationship. The development of trust in the research relationship is intertwined with the very practical issues of gaining consent, and maintaining confidentiality and anonymity. We consider the meaning of consent and how reliable consent can be established. The extent to which confidentiality and anonymity can be maintained within the research processes is debated and examples given. We discuss data protection and conclude the chapter by highlighting the factors that can generate mistrust.

Chapter 5 begins with the key issue of how to deal with ethical dilemmas when they arise. We return to principle ethics and show how they can be applied in practice to assist in resolving dilemmas. Additional frameworks for determining the best course of action when dilemmas arise are described. The chapter continues by focusing on the decisions that have to be made when planning research. Researchers are guided through the ethics of deciding on a research topic, choosing a methodology, the representation of data, recruitment, debriefing, feedback and aftercare, and the ethical demands of each stage are discussed. In the last part of this chapter we consider the external safeguards and opportunities for consultation that need to be in place to ensure ethical soundness at each stage of the process.

Chapter 6 discusses the ethical review systems in the UK and considers the processes of applying to ethical committees. We begin by outlining the development of research ethics committees and their roles and functions are discussed and critiqued. We focus on the ethical approval systems that operate in universities and in the National Health Service, as these are the two systems that counselling, nursing and social work researchers are most likely to encounter. We also include a section on making an ethical application to conduct research with offenders later in the chapter. We highlight the issues that are of most concern to ethical committees and provide guidance on making an application. Particular emphasis is placed on the practicalities involved in the preparation and submission of the application and the ingredients for producing an effective research proposal are outlined.

The final chapter considers the ethics relating to the social and political dimensions of research. It argues that the researcher has enduring responsibilities in relation to their research participants, the organisations they may be involved with and society at large. We emphasise the need to close the research circle by ensuring that research findings are disseminated appropriately and the ethical dilemmas that may arise in relation to dissemination are discussed. Accustomed to the bounds of confidentiality and individual work, counsellors and psychotherapists are often wary of becoming engaged at societal and political levels. This wider level of ethical responsibility, to disseminate the results of research and make any significant new understandings known to social policy makers and the media, is highlighted and discussed.

Throughout the book we include accounts from researchers on their ethical dilemmas and experiences as they engage with the research process. We have anonymised the accounts where ethically appropriate, and some of them are composites. However, the essence of the stories is accurate and they portray real experiences and dilemmas. We also provide examples of some of the materials that researchers will need to produce to ensure that their participants are fully informed and consulted. We hope that researchers will find them useful when they are creating their own research materials.

We both enjoy engaging in research and teaching research and research ethics. We are very aware that the counselling, health and social work professions need a stronger research base to maintain and develop their positions, and this is especially important in times of economic constraint. We are also aware of significant gaps in knowledge that need to be filled by sound ethical research and we hope that by reducing anxieties about ethical research practice we may enthuse practitioners to embark on more challenging projects.

Reference

Kant, I. (1993 [1785]). *Grounding for the Metaphysics of Morals* (3rd edition). Indianapolis, IN: Hackett Publishing Company.

1

The researcher: researching and developing ourselves

Researchers usually have an idea for a research project or an area for exploration in place at the start of their research study and in the initial stages tend to focus on refining these ideas. We would argue that attending to ethics is an equally important factor that needs consideration at the beginning of any research study, and we recommend that researchers start this process by reflecting on themselves. This chapter focuses on how researchers can develop their ethical sensitivity in order to achieve a sound basis for ethical practice in relation to others. The usefulness of codes of conduct and ethical guidelines in helping the researcher to achieve ethical competence is considered, and we give an overview of the theoretical basis for ethical research practice. We hope that it will give readers an understanding of the theories that underpin research ethics and the practical decisions that they will be making. An integral part of heightening researchers' ethical awareness is ensuring that they are caring for themselves within the research process. Counsellors, nurses and social workers will be well aware that in order to care for others it is necessary to be proactive in maintaining self-care and this applies equally when conducting research.

We will begin by considering the meaning of ethics. Beauchamp and Childress (1994: 4) define ethics simply as 'a generic term for various ways of understanding and examining the moral life'. Slote (1995) provides a more descriptive definition. Ethics, according to Slote, encompasses a wide range of questions about what is good, right and/or virtuous, and questions of value: 'What kind of life is best for the individual and how ought one behave in regard to other individuals and society as a whole' (Slote, 1995: 721). Our aim is to be able to conduct research ethically but how do individual researchers achieve this? When attempting to behave ethically there is often an understandable desire for a set of rules that will tell us what to do.

Codes, guidelines, frameworks and principle ethics

Counselling, nursing and social work are relatively new professions and in recent decades they have moved towards attaining professional status. An important strand of this evolution has been the development of codes of conduct. These ethical guidelines set standards to ensure that professionals will be competent, trustworthy, refrain from the deception and exploitation of others, and contribute to the greater good through their work (Tjeltveit, 1999). Most caring professions have a basic code of ethics or an ethical framework and some, such as the British Association for Counselling and Psychotherapy (BACP) and the British Psychological Society (BPS), have developed separate ethical guidelines for research. Guidelines provide us with useful prompts and are usually based on principle ethics. At this stage it would be much easier for the reader if we said 'when you do research use this ethical code', but we are more ambitious in thinking that researchers need to understand the underpinnings of these codes and frameworks. We want to put ethics at the centre of the research process rather than treat it as an afterthought. In order to do this we are going to delve more deeply into principle ethics.

Principle ethics form the middle level of a five-level model of ethical reasoning developed by Kitchener and Kitchener (2009). This model provides a useful map of the different levels of ethical reasoning and we will take a closer look at it before returning to think about the usefulness of ethical guidelines and frameworks.

The first level of the model is the intuitive, immediate response of the individual's moral conscience, often experienced as the 'gut feeling', and is based upon moral upbringing and experience. Shillito-Clarke (2003) suggests that it is often a sound guide but it may not be adequate when there are time pressures or unusual circumstances. The second level consists of the specific laws and codes of conduct that shape and constrain behaviour, such as a professional ethical framework.

At the next level are principles, which are universal values of equal worth (Shillito-Clarke, 2003). This level is very useful in practical reasoning and forms the basis for most ethical frameworks and guidelines. Beauchamp and Childress (1994) have identified four principles that have a 'prima facie' validity. These are beneficence (do good), non-maleficence (do no harm), autonomy (respect for self-determination), and justice (fairness). Two further principles have been identified as integral to ethical reasoning and are useful additions. Shillito-Clarke (1996) adds Kitchener's (1984) principle of fidelity (faithfulness), which she identifies as important for forming and maintaining therapeutic relationships, and Meara, Schmidt and Day (1996) add veracity (truthfulness), as it is a fundamental ingredient in establishing trust between people.

The principle of beneficence involves taking positive action to do good and includes an obligation to act. Choosing research topics that are most likely to make a positive contribution to knowledge and being proactive in ensuring that research participants are properly debriefed are examples of beneficent acts. Non-maleficence is defined as an obligation to do no harm. This embraces issues of competence as well as ensuring that exploitation and the abuse of power do not occur in practice, research or professional dealings with others. Autonomy means ensuring the right of the other to self-determination. This applies to such aspects of research as ensuring informed choice and the identification and careful management of issues that may oppress or disadvantage participants. Justice, according to Meara et al. (1996), is primarily concerned with distributive justice, for example, ensuring sensitivity to inequalities, and attention to civil rights. Fidelity involves the obligation to be trustworthy and loyal within relationships and to ensure that disruptions of trust, such as inappropriate dual relationships, do not occur. Meara et al. (1996) describe veracity as truthfulness and cite Bok's (1989) argument that veracity is a foundation of human community. 'I can have different kinds of trust: that you will have my interest at heart, that you will do me no harm. But if I do not trust your word, can I have genuine trust …?' (Bok, 1989: 31). When making an ethical judgement, no principle is considered paramount. Principles are examined for their relevance to a particular situation and then weighed against each other. We will return to principle ethics in Chapter 5 where we will show how these ethical principles can be applied in practice to aid in solving ethical dilemmas.

The fourth level of the ethics model is ethical theory. There are, of course, a vast range of ethical theories but Kitchener and Kitchener (2009) identify the ethical theories that are especially useful to researchers. These are: natural law ethics, virtue theory, utilitarianism, deontology, and the ethics of care. Natural law ethics hold that morality is implicit in human nature and that ethical outcomes can be arrived at by reasoning. The Stoic form of natural law emphasises the equality of all human beings. Virtue theory maintains that the development of each person's moral capacity, rather than laws or sets of rules, forms the basis for ethical actions. Utilitarianism places emphasis on the outcomes of actions. If an action results in something beneficial, then it is judged to be morally good. Utilitarians also take the view that moral actions should produce the greatest good for the largest number of people. Deontology is the science of duty and its most famous proponent is Immanuel Kant. Kant argued that duty should be the guide for actions. He placed emphasis on the importance of motives and said that it is not the outcome of an action that matters but the motives of the person concerned. The ethics of care focus on the obligation to act with care towards others (Kitchener and Kitchener, 2009). This strand of ethics includes feminist ethics and the ethical theories that prioritise relationship and responsibilities towards others. It can be seen that each of these ethical theories has its strengths and each may be particularly relevant in certain situations. However, it is also evident that they are often in opposition to each other and deciding which theory should take precedence or how these theories can interact in ethical decision making is the concern of the fifth level of metaethics.

Model of ethical reasoning

Level 1. Immediate level: the intuitive response.

Level 2. Laws: ethical rules, codes, guidelines and frameworks.

Level 3. Principle ethics: beneficence, non-maleficence, justice, autonomy, fidelity, and veracity.

Level 4. Ethical theories: natural law ethics, virtue theory, utilitarianism, deontology, and the ethics of care.

Level 5. Metaethics: deciding which ethical theory takes precedence and how ethical theories might interact. (Kitchener and Kitchener, 2009)

Philosophical theory is a complex subject and we have given the briefest possible overview but we hope that it will act as a reminder of the basic ideas. For those who are interested in ethical theory and its relation to research, Kitchener and Kitchener (2009) provide a readable and more detailed guide.

Let us return to thinking about ethical guidelines and how helpful such guidelines are for researchers. In these guidelines, which are based on principle ethics, there is often a stronger focus on non-maleficence than on the other principles. Bond (2004) observes that the motivation for developing codes of ethics often arises from a concern to redress previous wrongs; they are developed primarily to avoid harm rather than to do good. This means that there is a defensive element to them and researchers will often check them to ensure that they are not doing anything wrong (O'Donahue and Mangold, 1996). Such codes can foster a tick-box approach and do not inspire or encourage in-depth ethical consideration.

So are these guidelines adequate and if we adhere to them will they ensure ethical research practice? On the positive side they form a basis for good practice and alert us to previously unconsidered aspects of ethical practice. They aim to protect the public and establish confidence in professionals and they underpin a pre-existing assumption on the part of the general population that professionals will behave ethically. However, ethical codes or guidelines may also have less admirable functions. They have been criticised as being too focused on the well-being of the professions and, as Bersoff (1994) notes, this is not surprising as they are usually generated by the professionals concerned. Ethical committees attempt to redress this problem by appointing lay people but they are often in a minority and Veatch (1989) argues that clients and key stakeholders should have a much greater degree of participation in the development of ethical standards. It is also important that if these codes are to cater for a diverse community, then this diversity must be represented on the committees and within the codes or guidelines. This point is emphasised by Pederson (1989), who warns that codes of ethics can inscribe the dominant culture. An often-stated aim is to protect the public, but do guidelines actually do this or is ethical behaviour generated from a different source?

[T]hey do little or nothing to protect the public. They tell us nothing, surely that we do not accept for ourselves as a result of how we understand the process of psychotherapy. As a psychotherapist I do not need a code of ethics to tell me not to exploit someone.... I do not do this because of my own personal ethics and because of my understanding of transference and of the power relationship between therapist and patient.

(Gordon, 1999: 35, 36)

Gordon firmly places the responsibility to behave ethically within the individual and argues that it cannot be imposed by external regulation. This means that fundamentally good research practice depends on individual researchers taking responsibility to treat others with care and it is not dependent on regularly consulting ethical codes. As Kitchener (1996: 369) says, 'No code can legislate goodness.' In other words, codes of conduct are not enough to ensure ethical practice. Moreover, interpreting such codes or guidelines is not a simple matter. At times it requires a good deal of ethical sensitivity and experienced researchers differ on how the principles and guidelines should be applied in particular situations (Corey, 1991). There is even concern expressed that strict adherence to codes of conduct may encourage unethical behaviour. 'They do little to develop or support the active independent critical judgement or discernment that should be associated with true moral responsibility. They may engender confusion, passivity, apathy and even immorality – the antithesis to ethical discourse and responsibility' (Pattison, 1999: 375). Lowenthal and Snell (1997) expand on this perspective. They underline Levinas's (1989) emphasis on the importance of putting the other first and highlight two consequences that follow from this position. If the other is to be put first, then a code of conduct cannot be put first as it provides us with the wrong conceptual starting point. Secondly, they say that codes of conduct militate against being thoughtful about practice.

Bond (2005: 9) places codes of conduct in a useful perspective. He argues against rules 'becoming too dominant as a method of constructing ethics'. As an external authority, codes of conduct demand compliance and weaken the capacity of the researcher to develop an individual sense of ethical responsibility. However, Bond feels that a basic code of conduct is necessary and that it can provide a springboard for the individual practitioner to develop ethical mindfulness. He describes ethical mindfulness as a heightened awareness of the interplay between externally imposed ethics (extrinsic ethics) and individual ethical values (intrinsic ethics).

It is also important to recognise that ethical opinion is not a static entity. What is considered to be good ethical practice at one point in time may be viewed very differently twenty years later. Ethics are subject to transformation and our views on morality change as new challenges are met and we appreciate the complexities of our rules and regulations at a deeper level. Ethical guidelines have to be regularly reviewed in order to reflect changing times and mores.

A more positive view is that research guidelines and codes of conduct have served the purpose of raising the level of ethical discourse within the caring professions. However, it can be argued that the ethical principles that underpin codes and guidelines are themselves value-laden. Principle ethics have been developed from the Western individualistic tradition and have attracted criticism in their application to other cultural settings. The emphasis on the principle of autonomy, it is argued, is inappropriate for non-Western cultures where the well-being of the family or group is considered to be more important than that of the individual (Varma, 1988).

Principle ethics are also criticised from a feminist perspective by Rave and Larsen (1995), who assert that the feeling-intuitive dimension is under-emphasised. Gilligan (1982) supports the view that subjective feelings should be given a greater emphasis, and argues that intuition is a significant factor in the decision-making process. Robson et al. (2000) suggest that a rationalisation of actions takes place after the intuitive decision has been made, creating the illusion that a logical process has been followed. Their view is that the role of intuition should be fully acknowledged and balanced by opening the decision-making process to the scrutiny of peers and the public.

It is also evident that principle ethics focus on dilemmas and quandaries. In their ground-breaking paper, Meara et al. (1996) argue that professional ethics encompass more than just moral actions. Principle ethics emphasise the obligations of practitioners. Meara et al. argue that individuals should have ideals to which they aspire and they say that this 'ethical gap' can be filled by virtue ethics. We should develop our ability to engage morally with others rather than focusing on complying with rules. The key here is 'to aspire to the ideal'.

Virtue ethics

Rather than just seeking an external source of guidance for our actions, we need to develop our own capacity for ethical behaviour and reasoning. MacIntyre (1981) has made a significant contribution to the contemporary study of ethics by refocusing philosophical thought on the Aristotelian idea of virtues. Virtue ethics emphasises people's ethical characteristics (such as prudence, fortitude, integrity) rather than ethical principles, their dilemma-solving capacity or individual behaviour. However, Meara et al. (1996) do not want to discard principle ethics. They argue that virtue ethics complement principle ethics and should be integrated with them. For Meara et al. (1996: 24), the addition of virtue ethics 'calls upon individuals to aspire toward ideals and to develop virtues or traits of character that enable them to achieve these ideals'. They propose five attributes of virtuous agents (for our purposes, researchers). These are: motivation to do good; possession of vision and discernment; ability to realise the role of affect or emotion in assessing or judging proper conduct; having a high degree of self-understanding or awareness; and understanding the importance of community and diversity in moral decision making. They suggest the four virtues of prudence, integrity, respectfulness and benevolence as important ways of being for practitioners. These virtues form their profile of the virtuous professional. Meara et al. (1996) relate prudence and integrity to the goal of competence; and respectfulness and benevolence to the development of practice that is sensitive to all cultures, difference and the common good.

MacIntyre (1981) regards the development of virtues as not just an individual endeavour. He emphasises the role of the community in shaping virtues, an approach which contrasts with the individual development and other forms of individualism that are more familiar to Western cultures. This shaping of virtues by the community makes virtue ethics more relevant than principle ethics for ethical discussions in multicultural settings (Jordan and Meara, 1990).

The emphasis on the development of virtues adds strength to the previous arguments that we cannot just rely on a set of rules or guidelines to ensure that we are conducting ethical research. Before embarking on a research project we need to look more deeply within ourselves and ask the question 'What are the virtues that I personally need to develop in order to be a good researcher and how can they be achieved?' The emphasis that virtue ethics place on individual integrity brings to mind the idea of vocation. Vocation derives from the Latin verb *vocare*, to be called, and has been primarily associated with having a religious or spiritual calling. These days, the emphasis in many workplaces is on competencies, skills, targets and professional status. The word 'vocation' sounds rather old-fashioned and is rarely mentioned. Recently, Bennett (2005) has sought to revive this concept. 'Perhaps we need to rekindle our notion of professionalism more in line with a sense of vocation and calling, away from career, status and material rewards' (Bennett, 2005: 155). The basis of his argument is similar to Strawbridge's (2002) views on the 'McDonaldisation' of counselling, where she argues that counselling is being reduced from a social movement to a service delivery enterprise and, in the process, is in danger of becoming detached from its moral and ethical values. Although the word 'vocation' may not be much used these days, when asked what being a professional means to them, people in the caring professions often talk about it in ways that link it primarily to moral values (Danchev, 2006). In Box 1.1 Safia, a social worker, tells us what being a professional means to her.

BOX 1.1   BEING A PROFESSIONAL

Being a professional means to me that I have a particular relationship to others and the world that I live in. It's not just a qualification. It's not something that I put on when I go into work and leave there when I go home. You certainly don't become a social worker for money or status. It's about having a set of beliefs about people and the way that the world impacts on them. It's about how I relate to people. It affects everything I do. It's a core part of me. When I do research, that ingrained way of being informs my decisions and how I act. You can't get that from reading a list of rules. It has to be inside you.

Safia, a social worker.

Safia's view of what it means to be a professional also highlights the fact that the people who decide to become members of the caring professions and undergo training already possess the virtues that are necessary for ethical research practice. The issue is can these pre-existing virtues be brought more into the foreground and honed in ways that will ensure they are applied effectively to research practice? A related question is: are there ways of thinking about the world that need to be understood more fully in order to research effectively?

Developing an ethical approach to research

The view that researchers can assume an objective position in relation to their research is widely disputed (Willig, 2001). Whether quantitative or qualitative approaches are taken, the researcher has an agenda and a perspective. It is not possible to be neutral. The researcher can strive for a position of neutrality but realistically perhaps the best that can be achieved is to understand their own standpoint as fully as possible and to be transparent about it. Having become aware of their standpoint, it is then necessary to consider how this may influence the research agenda and attempt to balance this bias. If we are not aware of the ways in which our own values impact on our research, we are likely to produce distorted findings. As Pessoa says, 'What we see is not what we see but who we are' (Pessoa, 1991: 76). There are two major aspects to this process. The first is to gain an understanding of the impact and biases of our own worldview and the second is to try to understand the motivational forces that have led us to research a particular topic.

Researchers' values

We need to become aware of our own sets of values and these sets of values are often underpinned by ethical theories of which we are usually unaware. May (1984) describes these theories as underground root systems. Much of the ethical theory by which we operate at personal and professional levels is implicit and unacknowledged. These rarely examined ethics can be subtly conveyed in our language, behaviour and practices, and we may be so widely or deeply embedded in a particular culture that they remain unnoticed (Tjeltveit, 1999). In the unaware state, we often consider that the rules that we live by and the givens of our own way of life are the default position and regard the practices of others as strange, unusual or even wrong in some way. So a first step is to think about the context of our own lives and to attempt to view ourselves from a distance, to try to see ourselves as others see us. The aim is to move to the position of being able to see ourselves as 'other' and recognise our own 'strangeness'.

When we have gained an understanding of our own standpoint the next step is to be transparent about it so that readers of our research can assess our findings in the light of it being researched from a particular perspective. They can then make a judgement as to whether we have been successful in balancing any possible biases.

Researchers' motivation

Another aspect of the importance of increasing our self-knowledge relates to our choice of research topic. Why do individual researchers choose to explore particular subject areas? The reasons may be relatively benign, for example, the topic may fascinate us, we may have noticed a gap in our profession's knowledge base, or we may have been alerted to the need for deeper understanding by some aspect of our practice. However, we may be drawn to a topic because we feel passionately about it. This can stem from a personal experience or a deep feeling that previous researchers are wrong and we may want to prove that we are right about an issue. The latter types of attachment to a project can be problematic if individual motivations have not been thoroughly explored. Of course we may not be conscious of the depth of our motivation. A revealing test is to ask yourself how you would feel if you had to change topic. Do you feel relatively calm and relaxed about the change or does it evoke strong feelings? Unexplored motivations can have a significant negative impact, as is evident from the experience of the research supervisor described in Box 1.2.

BOX 1.2 THE UNCONSCIOUS ATTACHMENT

I was supervising Mike, a social work student, who had reached the writing-up phase of his Master's dissertation. At a personal level Mike was informed, insightful and worked to all required deadlines, and so we had established a good supervisory relationship. However, when it came to cutting his data down to fit within the parameters of his dissertation, Mike became defensive and argued over every line, even though his dissertation was 5,000 words over the 20,000 limit. It became clear that Mike's research area on the impact of school bullying had touched an unacknowledged part of himself and his story. This had been his unconscious motivation to research this particular area. Mike felt that to take out any words from his research participants' data would be to undervalue them and repeat a form of bullying; it would feel that their words were not being heard, believed or valued. I insisted on some cuts and while Mike successfully passed his dissertation, he never really forgave me for being 'too brutal'. In a parallel process, I think I too came to be viewed as a bully.

Personal knowledge of a subject area, and even passionate feelings, are not necessarily linked to poor research. Insider knowledge can be a great asset as it can enhance and inform the research, but it is probably harder work. It can demand a good deal of personal strength to understand how personal experience may distort and influence the research and to ensure that a balanced approach is maintained. It is necessary to keep asking oneself the question 'How is my past experience influencing how I am conducting this research?' Researchers may well be adept at self-reflection and their insider knowledge can be a valuable asset as it can sensitise them into asking deeper and more pertinent research questions. However, researching emotionally-charged topics can be exhausting so it is important to factor in the extra time, space and the support network needed for effective self-care while conducting the research.

Reflexivity

Closely tied to understanding individual standpoints and motivations is the concept of reflexivity. Reflexivity is not always well defined in the literature and sometimes it is used synonymously with reflection. Reflexivity is the ability to observe, assess and comment on the impact that we have on our research and the impact that our research has on us. We do this through reflection but it is a deep form of reflection where we take the usual, the normal, the given, and attempt to view them from different perspectives. When researching it is important to factor in time to consider proposed actions thoroughly. This also involves creating an internal reflective space where the emotional pulls and influences to which we are subject can be observed. This should not be done in a punitive way but with a supportive gentle approach that is underpinned by an awareness that we are trying to do our best in the circumstances in which we find ourselves.

Shillito-Clarke (2010) and Bond (2000) both refer to ethical mindfulness. They encourage us to approach every aspect of our research with ethical questions in the foreground. Shillito-Clarke (2010) speaks of ethical mindfulness as being consciously aware of our values and routinely asking moral questions of ourselves, our practice and our professional relationships. It is sort of ethical minesweeping of our actions and can be regarded as part of the reflexive process. How can we develop this practice and use it in a balanced way? It is a little like resetting our ethical thermostat. This comes about by understanding that almost every action of our lives encompasses an ethical element and monitoring how our behaviour and actions impact on others. Rather than a set of skills to be learned, it is a state of being that needs continuous attention.

Another means of strengthening our reflexive practice is to increase our sensitivity to the feelings and circumstances of others; to develop our capacity for empathy. Researchers with therapeutic training will already be skilled in this. It involves being able to see the world from the perspective of another person. The classic metaphor is to be able to walk in the other person's shoes. Empathy is important from an ethical perspective because it heightens our awareness of the experience of others and we are more likely to respond appropriately and sensitively if we have an in-depth understanding of their viewpoint. Perhaps the most important aspect of empathy in relation to reflexive practice is that by being able to view the world more accurately from the perspective of our participants, it alerts us to the nature of our own world view and how this might impact on our research.

For researchers, Halpern's conceptualisation of empathy as an engaged curiosity is useful. It 'involves a real interest in going beyond surface emotions and easy sympathetic identifications' (Halpern, 2012: 237). She recommends cultivating genuine curiosity and non-verbal attentiveness. The arts are also useful in widening our capacity for empathy. As Ricoeur (1984) says, artistic work extends an invitation to the reader or audience to occupy a world. Through engagement with books, film, drama and the arts in general, we can come to understand more deeply the emotions and dilemmas of human existence that we have not personally encountered. The sculptor Antony Gormley crystallises this effect by describing the arts and literature as 'instruments of reflexivity' (Gormley, 2011).

Balancing the biases

Having identified our standpoint and developed our reflexive capacity, how can preconceptions and biases be balanced? The concept of 'bracketing' can be a useful way of approaching this task. Bracketing was first suggested by Husserl, who argued that if we are to see and experience phenomena in their purest form, we have to set aside our preconceptions and existing knowledge of those things in order to see them anew. Whether it is possible to set aside these preconceptions has been contested by Heidegger and other philosophers. Whether it is theoretically possible is not something we are going to debate here, but we do think that the endeavour of setting aside prior knowledge and biases can be useful in practice. Rolls and Relf (2006) argue that this cannot be a one-off process that happens at the beginning of research; it ideally continues throughout the process. There needs to be an active attitude of and commitment to openness to learning from the data, a preparedness to change our views and to be modified by the research process. This applies equally to quantitative and qualitative research methods. Tufford and Newman (2012) suggest that the following activities may be helpful in aiding the process of identifying and setting aside or balancing our biases: keeping a reflexive diary, reflective interviews and memoing.

Keeping a research diary aids self-reflection. Begin it by writing down what you expect the research findings to be and then monitor how the process impacts on you and changes your perspective. If you reach the end of the study and your findings exactly match those you initially proposed, then it is possible that you have not managed to set aside your own perspective on the subject. Research journals are a particularly useful means of gaining insight into biases. By writing down our thoughts and feelings we externalise them and can then view them from this different perspective, which can be helpful in enabling us to identify predispositions and distortions in our thinking.

A valuable resource in this endeavour is other people. Reflective interviews can be arranged with a colleague or other trusted person who can challenge the way we are thinking about our research process. The person may be a research supervisor(s), colleague, fellow student, friend or family member. Ensure that there is a relationship with at least one other person with whom it is possible to feel safe in expressing unformed thoughts. Speaking our thoughts out loud also enables us to hear our own words and reflect on them more deeply.

Tufford and Newman's third suggestion is utilising the grounded theory method of memoing. Memos are a means of capturing research-related thoughts that occur as we are working on specific parts of the research process. So, for example, while we are collecting data we may think that particular patterns are emerging that may suggest causal relationships. These thoughts are captured in a separate notebook and kept for later reflection when they can be reviewed and tested against the data. If they turn out to be wrong, it could indicate that we were hoping for a particular outcome. Reflecting on why this might be can be revealing.

It can be said that throughout the research process we are not only researching a chosen topic but are also researching ourselves. These active ways of reflecting on ourselves ensure that we are taking as ethical an approach as possible to our research. As well as trying to develop our capacity for becoming ethical researchers, it is also worth considering the types of unethical behaviour that may occur in research. What are the pitfalls that need to be avoided?

What might cause us to act unethically?

Even though we may strive to do our best, it is part of the human condition that we will make mistakes and the most common form of unethical behaviour stems from errors. The philosopher Popper (1996) firmly rejects the idea that mistakes are avoidable. In accepting that mistakes will occur, the unethical action is to cover them up as this prevents learning from taking place. The hiding of mistakes is the 'greatest intellectual sin' and the ethical duty is to be open about them (Popper, 1996: 202). Unfortunately, unethical behaviour is not restricted to mistakes. Palmer Barnes (1998) draws our attention to three additional forms: poor practice, negligence and malpractice. Poor practice often results from not possessing the adequate skills needed to conduct a particular form of research, or rushing into a study without good preparation. Negligence is about failing to ensure that no harm comes to others, either through ignorance or from other motivations. Malpractice involves committing active misdemeanours such as falsifying data, misrepresenting research findings, making erroneous claims, or exploiting participants. It can result from external pressures to produce results as well as from individual career and/or financial motivations.

Serious research malpractice is relatively rare and unethical behaviour in research stems more often from more usual pressures. If studying for a degree, time may be short and the temptation to cut corners arises. The pressure to produce a thesis or research dissertation by a particular deadline and of an acceptable quality can lead to behaviour such as the falsification of data through panic, the recruitment of friends or close colleagues as participants, or the distortion of analyses to make the results more interesting. Unethical behaviour may also result from a fear of failure or a fantasy of rejection. This can manifest itself through a reluctance to ask people to participate or a failure to ask for help and guidance when it is needed.

Other forms of organisational pressure may contribute to misrepresenting research. An important factor in the professionalisation of the helping professions has been the establishment of an evidence base, and in recent years economic constraints and the allied struggle for survival may have added pressure to produce 'hard' evidence for efficacy and efficiency. This can create ethical dilemmas, as the manager of a workplace counselling service found in the example given in Box 1.3.

BOX 1.3   THE TEMPTATION TO CREATE DATA

When I was appointed to the post of manager of the counselling service, I had had no managerial experience. It came as a shock to me to realise that probably the most important part of my job was defending the service against financial cuts. Almost every time a counsellor's contract was due to be renewed I would have to justify its renewal. A similar thing would happen if one of the permanent staff left. I quickly became adept at gathering hard data to underpin my arguments for maintaining the staffing levels. One year the client numbers dropped and the temptation to add a few more sessions

---

into the statistics was enormous. I didn't actually do it, but it was very hard to resist, especially if you knew that it was likely that a contract would not be renewed as a result of that year's stats. I remember sitting at my desk agonising over it. I was very aware what the loss of a job would mean to the people concerned. They were my colleagues and friends.

Responsibilities towards self

A good deal of thinking about research ethics focuses on acting in the best interests of others, but it is equally important to include ourselves in this deliberation. If you are not in a good physical and mental state, then you will probably not do your best work. Cramming four interviews into one day is not only likely to produce poor data, but it is also going to take its toll on you. Being in good condition to do your best work is also about respecting your participants. They are giving up their time and providing you with information and they deserve the best from you. Attention to self-care is an important part of ethical practice.

There are also more serious aspects of self-care to consider. Before commencing any project it is essential to think about whether you might be at risk in any way by conducting this research. Several areas need particular consideration. These are researcher safety, researcher traumatisation, and researcher guilt and shame.

Researcher safety

The practical aspects of safety need to be borne in mind when planning and conducting research. For example, are you recruiting from a completely unknown population or exploring a subject where particular risks may be encountered? Do you need to ensure that contact with participants takes place in a safe environment? Do you need to have another person present, nearby or aware of your whereabouts? The degree of protection that you need to have in place will depend on the subject of your research, but whatever you are researching your own safety and that of your participants needs to be carefully considered. The checklist in Box 1.4 will help you to think these issues through.

BOX 1.4   RESEARCHER SAFETY CHECKLIST

Do you understand the extent of your own connections to the subject you are researching?

Have you had adequate training to deal with sensitive or emotional material?

(Continued)

(Continued)

Have you arranged to meet participants in a safe environment?

Do you need another person to accompany you?

Do you need to have an alarm system?

Have you told a reliable person about your whereabouts?

Do you have some form of debriefing in place?

Can you contact a supportive person as and when needed?

Will your research be disseminated in a way that will address your participants' issues?

Researcher traumatisation

When you gaze long into an abyss the abyss also gazes into you.

(Nietzsche, 1990: 102)

Nietzsche's warning may feel a little extreme to prospective researchers. Counsellors, nurses and social workers generally have good empathic qualities and are skilled at gaining a deep understanding of their clients' lived experience. In relation to research, this is good in that the description and understanding of the participants' concerns will be faithful and of a high quality, but it also means that researchers may be more vulnerable to secondary traumatisation. It has also been suggested that an ethic of commitment can expose researchers to feelings of stress (Reinharz, 1992). Counsellors, nurses and social workers may have a deep commitment to improve the lives of participants through undertaking a particular research project. This is admirable, but it is important to be aware that really good support systems for the researcher need to be in place before the research has started. There is also evidence that exploring the lived experience of traumas, such as sexual abuse or domestic violence, can impact negatively on researchers (Coles and Mudaly, 2010; Fontes, 2004). Common emotional responses experienced included anger, guilt, shame, fear, sadness, crying and feelings of depression. Symptoms more closely associated with trauma, such as nightmares, intrusive thoughts, fear, anger, irritability and difficulty concentrating, have also been reported (Coles et al., 2010).

A good subject for future research would be to consider whether being a member of the counselling, nursing or social work professions increases vulnerability to researcher traumatisation. In their daily practice these researchers will have seen a lot more in terms of extreme human behaviour and distress. In a variety of ways they have already stared into the abyss and studying a potentially traumatic subject area may be adding to the existing load.

Additionally, the nature of the research process itself can be inherently stressful. There are times of overload when there are deadlines to meet and moments when errors occur, such as erasing digital interviews or losing data sets through computer failure. There are also equally stressful periods of time when nothing much seems to be happening. A lesser but more subtle form of negative experience may also occur. The treasured assumptions of the researcher are often called into question as the research progresses and letting go of a deeply held viewpoint can be an uncomfortable and disorienting experience.

On the positive side researchers will probably have had some form of therapeutic or mental health training and will be more likely to notice changes in themselves and seek help. Post-traumatic stress research indicates that not everyone has the same response to exposure to traumatic material or events. The degree of impact depends on factors such as the intensity of the trauma, the length and frequency of exposure to it, the researcher's personal history and the quality of the support network that is available to them (Hetherington, 2001).

Prevention is better than post-event remedies. At the beginning ensure that there is someone you can talk to about the emotional impact of the research. This may be your supervisor or colleague or someone else that you trust. It is good practice to have some form of debriefing in place so that you can work through any difficult feelings that remain. At times the nature of the project is such that professional support may be needed, as is evident from the experience of the researcher related in Box 1.5.

BOX 1.5   DIRECT OBSERVATION OF TRAUMATIC EVENTS CAN HAVE RISKS

Early in my counselling career I was a research assistant on a project that explored stress in firefighters. The study included observation of operational work and I attended several incidents that involved fatalities. One incident involved the death of a person in the back of a car. For several months afterwards I had flashbacks while driving my car and experienced feelings of panic when getting into the back of a friend's car. As I knew beforehand that I would be experiencing some traumatic incidents, I had arranged regular counselling with a psychiatrist and he helped me to make the connection that explained why this particular incident had affected me so deeply. Many years earlier, a close relative had died suddenly in the back of a car and this prior event was unconsciously connecting with the research incident. Once I understood what was happening, the symptoms began to diminish and they eventually completely resolved.

The above example clearly shows how a researcher may be traumatised by their experiences and how their personal history can connect unconsciously to the trauma. It also shows that the impact of these experiences can be lessened by having effective support in place.

Researcher guilt and shame

Guilt and shame can be felt when there is a sharp difference between the circumstances of the researcher and their participants. Common factors are poverty, disease or danger. The researcher is in the position of witnessing and can feel powerless when brought face to face with inequalities and iniquities. The resulting feelings of guilt and shame can be mitigated by a conviction that the research is needed and will make a difference (Campbell, 2002). If we are exploring sensitive issues without a clear commitment to disseminating the results in a fashion that will ultimately benefit participants, then we may be vulnerable to feelings of guilt and shame. Occasionally, feelings of shame and guilt evoked by research activity may have deeper roots that go beyond the particular piece of research we are engaged in, and it may require professional help to explore the origins of these feelings.

Conclusion

In this chapter we have explored the meaning of ethics. Research codes of ethics and guidelines are based on important philosophical principles designed to act as a guide to ensure that our research is beneficial to others as well as to ourselves. However, it is clear that research codes and guidelines are not enough to ensure ethical behaviour. Who we are is the crucial factor. In particular, it is essential to understand the context within which we have developed our own view of the world and recognise how this standpoint might influence the research process. By enhancing self-awareness and our reflexive skills, we can increase our openness to new perspectives. Finally, we have emphasised that self-care is an integral and very necessary part of the ethical research process if we are to produce the best possible research. In the next chapter we are going to look at the research experience from the other side and explore what it means to be a participant.

REFLECTIVE QUESTIONS

- What is motivating you to explore this particular research topic?
- How might this choice of subject impact on you?
- What do you consider to be the most important virtues for a researcher to develop?
- When you read your profession's code or guidelines for research ethics what were your reflections?
- What personal safety issues do you need to consider in relation to your research?
- If any of your reflections raise ethical concerns, who could you talk to about this?

References

Beauchamp, T.L. and Childress, J.F. (1994). *Principles of Biomedical Ethics* (4th edition). New York: Oxford University Press.

Bennett, M. (2005). *The Purpose of Counselling and Psychotherapy*. Basingstoke: Palgrave Macmillan.

Bersoff, D.N. (1994). Explicit ambiguity: the 1992 ethics code as oxymoron. *Professional Psychology: Research and Practice*, 25(4): 382–387.

Bok, S. (1989). *Common Values*. Columbia, MO: University of Missouri Press.

Bond, T. (2000). *Standards and Ethics for Counselling in Action*. London: Sage.

Bond, T. (2004). An introduction to the ethical guidelines for counselling and psychotherapy. *Counselling and Psychotherapy Research*, 4(2): 4–9.

Bond, T. (2005). Developing and monitoring professional ethics and good practice guidelines. In R. Tribe and J. Morrissey (Eds.), *Handbook of Professional and Ethical Practice*. Hove: Brunner-Routledge.

Campbell, R. (2002). *Emotionally Involved*. London: Routledge.

Coles, J., Dartnall, E., Limjerwala, S. and Astbury, J. (2010). *Researcher Trauma, Safety and Sexual Violence Research. Briefing Paper: Sexual Violence Research Initiative*. Accessed on 20 October 2012 at www.svri.org/takingcare.pdf.

Coles, J. and Mudaly, N. (2010). Staying safe: strategies for qualitative child abuse researchers. *Child Abuse Review*, 19(1): 56–69.

Corey, G. (1991). *Theory and Practice of Counseling and Psychotherapy* (4th edition). Pacific Grove, CA: Brooks Cole.

Danchev, D. (2006). Counselling psychologists' perspectives on professionalism. Unpublished DPsych thesis, City University, London.

Fontes, L.A. (2004). Ethics in violence against women research: the sensitive, the dangerous, and the overlooked. *Ethics and Behaviour*, 14(2): 141–174.

Gilligan, C. (1982). *In a Different Voice*. Cambridge, MA: Harvard University Press.

Gordon, P. (1999). *Face to Face: Therapy as Ethics*. London: Constable.

Gormley, A. (2011). Interview. *BBC News*, 13 August 2011.

Halpern, J. (2012). Clinical empathy in medical care. In J. Decety (Ed.), *Empathy: From Bench to Bedside*. Cambridge, MA: MIT Press.

Hetherington, A. (2001). *The Use of Counselling Skills in Emergency Services*. Buckingham: Open University Press.

Jordan, A.E. and Meara, N.M. (1990). The role of virtues and principles in moral collapse: a response to Miller. *Professional Psychology: Research and Practice*, 22: 107–109.

Kitchener, K.S. (1984). Intuition, critical evaluation and ethical principles: the foundation for ethical decisions in counselling psychology, *The Counselling Psychologist*, 12(3): 43–55.

Kitchener, K.S. (1996). Professional codes of ethics and on-going moral problems in psychology. In W. O'Donohue and R.F. Kitchener (Eds.), *The Philosophy of Psychology*. London: Sage.

Kitchener, K.S. and Kitchener, R.F. (2009). Social science research ethics: historical and philosophical issues. In D.M. Mertens and P.E. Ginsberg (Eds.), *The Handbook of Social Research Ethics*. Los Angeles, CA: Sage.

Levinas, E. (1989). Ethics as first philosophy. In S. Hand (Ed.), *The Levinas Reader*. Oxford: Blackwell.

Loewenthal, D. and Snell, R. (1997). The ethical postmodern counsellor. Paper given at the BPS Division of Counselling Psychology Conference, Stratford upon Avon, England, May.

MacIntyre, A. (1981). *After Virtue: A Study in Moral Theory*. London: Duckworth.

May, W.F. (1984). The virtues in a professional setting. *Soundings*, 67(3): 245–266.

Meara, N.M., Schmidt, L.D. and Day, J.D. (1996). Principles and virtues: A foundation for ethical decisions, policies and character. *The Counseling Psychologist*, 24(1): 4–77.

Nietzsche, F. (1990). *Beyond Good and Evil*. London: Penguin.

O'Donahue, W. and Mangold, R. (1996). A critical examination of the ethical principles of psychologists and code of conduct. In W. O'Donohue and R.F. Kitchener (Eds.), *The Philosophy of Psychology*. London: Sage.

Palmer Barnes, F. (1998). *Complaints and Grievances in Psychotherapy: A Handbook of Ethical Practice*. London: Routledge.

Pattison, S. (1999). Are professional codes ethical? *Counselling*, 10(5): 374–380.

Pederson, P. (1989). Developing multicultural ethical guidelines for psychology. *International Journal of Psychology*, 24: 643–652.

Pessoa, F. (1991). *The Book of Disquiet*. London: Serpent's Tail.

Popper, K. (1996). *Toleration and Intellectual Responsibility. In Search of a Better World: Lectures and Essays from Thirty Years*. Trans. Laura J. Bennett. London: Routledge.

Rave, E.J. and Larsen, C.C. (Eds.) (1995). *Ethical Decision Making in Therapy: Feminist Perspectives*. New York: Guilford Press.

Reinharz, S. (1992). *Feminist Methods in Social Research*. New York: Oxford University Press.

Ricoeur, P. (1984). *Time and Narrative*. Trans. Kathleen McLaughlin and David Pellauer. Chicago, IL: University of Chicago Press.

Robson, M., Cook, P., Hunt, K., Alred, G. and Robson, D. (2000). Towards ethical decision making in counselling research. *British Journal of Guidance and Counselling*, 28(4): 533–547.

Rolls, L. and Relf, M. (2006). Bracketing interviews: addressing methodological challenges in qualitative interviewing in bereavement and palliative care. *Mortality*, 11(3): 286–305.

Shillito-Clark, C. (1996). Ethical issues in counselling psychology. In R. Woolfe and W. Dryden (Eds.), *Handbook of Counselling Psychology*. London: Sage.

Shillito-Clarke, C. (2003). Ethical issues in counselling psychology. In R. Woolfe, W. Dryden and S. Strawbridge (Eds.), *Handbook of Counselling Psychology* (2nd edition). London: Sage.

Shillito-Clarke, C. (2010). Ethical issues in counselling psychology. In R. Woolfe, S. Strawbridge, B. Douglas and W. Dryden (Eds.), *Handbook of Counselling Psychology* (3rd edition). London: Sage.

Slote, M. (1995). Ethics: task of ethics. In W.T. Reich (Ed.), *Encyclopaedia of Bioethics* (2nd edition). New York: Macmillan.

Strawbridge, S. (2002). McDonaldisation or fast food therapy. *Counselling Psychology Review*, 17(4): 20–24.

Tjeltveit, A.C. (1999). *Ethics and Values in Psychotherapy*. London: Routledge.

Tufford, L. and Newman, P. (2012). Bracketing in qualitative research. *Qualitative Social Work*, 11: 80.

Varma, V.K. (1988). Culture, personality and psychotherapy. *International Journal of Social Psychiatry*, 34(2): 142–149.

Veatch, R.M. (1989). *Medical Ethics*. Boston, MA: Jones and Bartlett.

Willig, C. (2001). *Qualitative Research in Psychology*. Buckingham: Open University Press.

2

The participant: responsibility, care and consideration

In the early stages of a research project a good deal of energy is put into finding a research question and thinking about an appropriate methodology. Less attention is given to thinking about the people who might be participating in the research. We would like to suggest that during preparation as much time and attention goes into a consideration of the potential research participants as into the other areas. In this chapter we aim to raise researchers' awareness of their responsibilities in relation to participants and to understand more fully what it may mean to be in the position of a participant in their research project.

The labels

Throughout this book we are using the term 'participants' to describe people who have agreed to take part in research projects. In the early days of medical, psychological and social science research, people taking part in studies were viewed from the perspective of the researchers and other interested third parties. There was a tendency for them to be objectified and 'subjected' to research and the interests of others. Over time this perspective has been modified and the description of people who have agreed to participate in research has moved from 'research subject' to 'participant' and to 'co-researcher'. The use of these labels is important because they are not neutral. They position people and this impacts on both the participant and the approach of the researcher. People are research 'subjects' when their involvement in the research process is limited to that of respondents who answer questions developed by others, and where they have very limited power over the research process apart from deciding which information to convey or retain (Dona, 2007: 212). Consent is obtained on a one-off basis and usually involves signing a form. The description 'participant' conveys a sense of co-operative engagement and informed consent that is confirmed at several points in time. Participants are often consulted and involved in the development of the study; the right to withdraw from the study at any point up until final write-up and publication is emphasised; and they are sent details of the findings. This is the most usual position for the majority of people who engage in contemporary research studies. The term 'co-researcher' has become more widely used in recent years and, at its best, represents an optimal level of practice and respect (see Oliver, 1997). However it has also been used in a way that reduces it to labelling rather than a lived reality. If participants are to be called co-researchers, then that is exactly what they should be. They should be involved from the start of the project and consulted about the design, means of data collection, analysis, discussion and conclusions, and given equal listing in the credits if they are comfortable with waiving their anonymity. The term 'participant' is used in this book because we feel that it is applicable to the widest range of current research approaches and methodologies.

It is evident that the use of the terms relating to participants demands an awareness of the power relations that exist between the researcher and the researched. The positioning of the research participant and the degree of power that they have to influence the research process is highly significant and directly related to the ways in which people have been treated in the past. The historical background to research participation underlines the importance of attending carefully to participant agency.

History of participant research ethics

The focus on research ethics and the rights of research participants began with the Nuremberg trials in 1947 following the Second World War. During this war research experiments were carried out on people against their will. The most extreme examples of unethical research practices were found in the Nazi concentration and death camps. Auschwitz, for example, was the site of appalling medical experimentation by Josef Mengele, a Nazi doctor (US Holocaust Memorial Museum, 2012). The details that came to light during the 1947 trials produced profound revulsion that such things could occur and provided the impetus for the development of a set of rules to underpin ethical practice in medical research. The resulting Nuremberg Code is important because its influence has extended beyond the medical world and has formed the basis for modern research ethics. Annas and Grodin (2008) highlight its three main strengths. First, it is based on principles of natural law and human rights that have universal application. Secondly, it underlines the principle of informed consent and the right to withdraw consent should the participant so wish. Thirdly, it emphasises the obligations of researchers to protect participants' welfare. It is written in the language of its time and uses the word 'experiment' where today we would speak of 'research' (see Box 2.1).

The Nuremberg Code (1947)

The voluntary consent of the human subject is absolutely essential. This means that the person involved should have legal capacity to give consent; should be so situated as to be able to exercise free power of choice, without the intervention of any element of force, fraud, deceit, duress, over-reaching, or other ulterior form of constraint or coercion; and should have sufficient knowledge and comprehension of the elements of the subject matter involved as to enable him to make an understanding and enlightened decision. This latter element requires that before the acceptance of an affirmative decision by the experimental subject there should be made known to him the nature, duration, and purpose of the experiment; the method and means by which it is to be conducted; all inconveniences and hazards reasonable to be expected; and the effects upon his health or person which may possibly come from his participation in the experiment. The duty and responsibility for ascertaining the quality of the consent rests upon each individual who initiates, directs or engages in the experiment. It is a personal duty and responsibility which may not be delegated to another with impunity.

The experiment should be such as to yield fruitful results for the good of society, unprocurable by other methods or means of study, and not random and unnecessary in nature.

The experiment should be so designed and based on the results of animal experimentation and a knowledge of the natural history of the disease or other problem under study that the anticipated results will justify the performance of the experiment.

The experiment should be so conducted as to avoid all unnecessary physical and mental suffering and injury.

No experiment should be conducted where there is an a priori reason to believe that death or disabling injury will occur; except, perhaps, in those experiments where the experimental physicians also serve as subjects.

The degree of risk to be taken should never exceed that determined by the humanitarian importance of the problem to be solved by the experiment.

Proper preparations should be made and adequate facilities provided to protect the experimental subject against even remote possibilities of injury, disability, or death.

The experiment should be conducted only by scientifically qualified persons. The highest degree of skill and care should be required through all stages of the experiment of those who conduct or engage in the experiment.

During the course of the experiment the human subject should be at liberty to bring the experiment to an end if he has reached the physical or mental state where continuation of the experiment seems to him to be impossible.

During the course of the experiment the scientist in charge must be prepared to terminate the experiment at any stage, if he has probable cause to believe, in the exercise of the good faith, superior skill and careful judgment required of him that a continuation of the experiment is likely to result in injury, disability, or death to the experimental subject.

The Nuremberg Code aimed to protect against a repeat of the Nazi atrocities but, as Ashcroft notes, 'in the post-war period it became evident that unethical research was not merely a pathology of totalitarian regimes but could also be found in liberal democracies' (Ashcroft, 2008: 141). This chilling realisation resulted in further action. The World Medical Association, also founded in the post-war era, became aware of the pressing need to raise the ethical standard of research. In 1964, following discussions at a meeting in Finland, it produced the Helsinki Declaration (WMA, 1964). The Declaration has been amended several times since 1964 to keep pace with current thinking. It was last amended in 2008 and the latest version can be viewed at: www.wma.net/en/30publications/10policies/b3/index.html.

The Helsinki Declaration has international status and is regarded as the most influential document on research ethics for medicine and the allied professions. It has been integrated into the legal systems of many countries and should take precedence if it is found to be in conflict with national laws. The main criticism of it is that it takes a Western perspective and does not adequately address the needs of the developing world. It has also been found to contain 'internal contradictions and vagueness of statement' (Ashcroft, 2008: 147). However, its central purpose and value is to guide and inspire and to be of use for individual researchers and ethical committees.

Today most professional organisations in counselling, health and social work have a statement of research ethics contained within their ethical frameworks. A few have separate research ethics guidance. A list of website locations of the current versions can be found in Box 2.1.

BOX 2.1   RESEARCH ETHICS GUIDELINES AND FRAMEWORKS FOR COUNSELLING, NURSING AND SOCIAL WORK

Separate document on ethics for researchers:

British Association for Counselling and Psychotherapy – *Ethical Guidelines for Researching Counselling and Psychotherapy*
www.bacp.co.uk/research/ethical_guidelines.php

British Psychological Society – *Code of Human Research Ethics*

www.bps.org.uk/sites/default/files/documents/code_of_human_research_ethics.pdf

Specific section on research ethics contained within the main code of ethics:

British Association of Social Workers – *The Code of Ethics for Social Workers*

www.basw.co.uk/about/code-of-ethics/. See section 4.4.4.

Mention of research within the main code of ethics:

United Kingdom Council for Psychotherapy – *Ethical Principles and Code of Conduct*

www.psychotherapy.org.uk/hres/UKCP/Ethical-Principles-and-Code-of-Professional-Conduct-approved-by-BOT-Sept-2009.pdf. See sections 3.4 and 7.3

Despite the post-war emphasis on ethical research, contraventions of the modern guidelines have occurred. The Milgram obedience experiment (Milgram, 1974), and the 1971 Stanford Prison Experiment (Zimbardo, 1973) are well-known examples of an insufficient regard for the impact of the research process on participant welfare. They are often quoted in relation to research ethics and the care of participants and are summarised below (see Box 2.2 and Box 2.3).

BOX 2.2   THE MILGRAM OBEDIENCE EXPERIMENT (MILGRAM, 1974)

Milgram, a professor at Yale University, became fascinated by the Nazi war criminals' claim that when they committed atrocities they were 'just following orders'. He wanted to explore the degree to which people in the normal population would obey orders when it was clear that their actions were directly harming someone. Milgram recruited 40 participants via newspaper advertisements and each person was paid a fee for participating. The experiment consisted of each participant acting as a teacher who would give a student an electric shock when they gave the wrong answer to a question. The shock apparatus delivered shocks in an ascending order of severity up to and beyond levels that were clearly labelled as dangerous. Unknown to the participants, the shock machine was in fact completely harmless and the 'student' was a stooge who acted out extreme pain and distress on receiving the more extreme shocks. During the experiment, even though the 'student' claimed to have a heart disorder or demanded to be released, the experimenter would urge the participant to continue to administer shocks. Milgram predicted that few of the participants would administer the severer levels of shock but to his surprise 26 of the 40 participants completely obeyed the orders they were given. However, many of the participants became profoundly upset during the experiment. This study raised considerable concern about deception and the use of participants in research. Milgram felt that the experiment was valuable in developing understanding about how people can become complicit in sadistic acts. The experiment has been much criticised for its methods as well as for the way it used the participants (Parker, 2000).

BOX 2.3   THE STANFORD PRISON EXPERIMENT (ZIMBARDO, 1973)

Zimbardo's aim for this research was to discover more about the psychological impact of becoming a prisoner or a prison guard. Zimbardo and his team from Stanford University recruited 24 student participants and paid them a fee to take on the randomly assigned roles of prisoners and prison guards in a specially constructed prison in a university basement. The prison guards took to their roles with such enthusiasm that

(Continued)

(Continued)

they became psychologically abusive towards the prisoners to such an extent that the experiment had to be stopped prematurely. The conditions of the experiment had created an environment that placed the participants in an emotionally and psychologically damaging situation. As in the Milgram experiment, the methods were strongly criticised as well as the lack of care and concern for the welfare of the participants (Fromm, 1973).

These experiments occurred over forty years ago but there is no room for complacency. A significant transgression in medical research occurred as recently as the 1990s. In 1997 Lurie and Wolfe drew attention to the use of placebo-controlled trials in HIV research in the USA and developing countries. The research was investigating the effectiveness of a new drug in the prevention of the transmission of the HIV virus from mothers to their children. The non-USA participants in the placebo group were not provided with antiretroviral drugs at the end of the trial despite evidence to show that these were effective against transmission of the disease. This contrasted with the USA trials where all participants had access to antiretroviral drugs (Lurie and Wolfe, 1997).

Professional ethical frameworks in counselling, nursing and social work emphasise the principle of autonomy. The aim of this emphasis is to counteract the unequal power dynamics that exist within the caring relationship. Autonomy underpins an attitude of respect for the views of others but it can also have a dark side. Researchers can consciously or unconsciously use the concept of participant autonomy to side-step their own responsibilities. Participants can be assumed to have equal power and agency as a default position and this assumption leaves them with too great a share of the responsibility. Even when there are no clear vulnerabilities, sensitivity to the inequalities in power that can exist between participants and researchers is needed.

Although ethical guidelines raise awareness and provide an important underpinning for research practice, individual vigilance on the part of researchers is essential to ensure good practice. In particular, researchers need to sensitise themselves to their responsibilities in relation to research participants. The ethical thinking of Emmanuel Levinas helps us to gain a deeper understanding of our individual obligations to participants.

Levinas

How, then, should we view our responsibilities towards participants and how can these responsibilities be translated into practice? The question of the degree of responsibility we should have towards others was an enduring preoccupation for Emmanuel Levinas (1906–1995). Levinas was born in Lithuania, educated in Russia and attended university in France and Germany, where he studied under the philosophers Heidegger and Husserl. He became a French citizen in 1930 and was living in France at the time of the Nazi invasion. He was drafted into the French Army as a translator of German and Russian, was captured by the Germans in 1940 and sent to a military prison camp for the duration of the war. Fortunately, during this time his wife and daughter were kept hidden by nuns. Following the war, he felt 'dominated by the presentiment and memory of the Nazi horror' (Levinas, 1990 [1963]) and it had a deep impact on his philosophy. His experiences concentrated his thought on the degree of responsibility we should have for others and the impact that this has on the relationships between people. We will focus on the relationship between the researcher and the participant in more detail in the next chapter, but for the purposes of this chapter we will explore Levinas's ideas about responsibility.

Levinas argues that in our encounters with other people we are exposed to their 'face'. This can literally mean their face, but it can also mean their expression, body language, general demeanour or any means of communicating with us that is present. In an interview in the book *Is it Righteous to Be?* (Robbins, 2001), Levinas refers to a passage in the novel *Life and Fate* by Vasily Grossman (2006). Grossman is describing a queue in the Lubianka – the Soviet prison for political prisoners. This is a queue for people to hand over letters and gifts for prisoners. The people are frightened of the guards and Grossman describes the hunched shoulders of a terrified woman. This, according to Levinas, is an example of 'the face'. We have seen her hunched shoulders and understood her fear and her situation, and, having seen it, we become responsible for her. We are not responsible for causing her terror, but we have seen it. Levinas says that through this encounter with the 'face' we become responsible. We have seen the person in all their human vulnerability and whether we like it or not we are now beholden to them. As Levinas puts it, we are now their 'hostage'. Counsellors, nurses and social workers will be familiar with this form of encounter as often when we see vulnerability in another person we feel the need, the pull, the 'demand', to respond (Gordon, 1999). Levinas argues that in our encounters there is a pre-existing responsibility that we have for others; it is pre-eminent and it overrides all other things. Levinas asserted that ethical practice is encapsulated in this responsibility for the other. By 'responsibility', Levinas means being for the other and the 'being for' is unconditional. For Levinas, the face 'in a certain way, in its silence, it calls you. Your reaction to the face is a response. Not just a response but a responsibility' (Wright, Hughes and Ainley, 1988). Levinas's work is valuable because it heightens our awareness of our responsibilities towards others. For those who would like to know more about his ideas, Orange (2010) provides a readable introduction.

If we apply Levinas's thinking to our research participants, it becomes clear that we do not start from a neutral position in terms of responsibility towards them. We are responsible for our research participants from the moment we first encounter them. However, the question arises that if researchers are taking responsibility, is this also inadvertently disempowering participants? In his book, *Postmodern Ethics*, Bauman (1993) warns us that in taking responsibility for participants we must take care not to take responsibility away from them. Participants also have their responsibilities towards themselves and others, and facing our full responsibility for participants does not necessarily lead to their disempowerment. The two are not mutually exclusive. The balance has to be carefully considered and the key lies in striving for equitable power relations and the avoidance of paternalism.

In our consideration of our degree of responsibility towards participants, there is a further element to explore. Levinas emphasises that we should put the other before ourselves.

In practical terms this means that the well-being of the participant is more important than our research project; it is more important than our qualification or degree; and it is more important than the knowledge that we may gain by undertaking research. If there is anything in our actions that might cause discomfort or distress to participants it should be remedied, even if this is detrimental to our research endeavours. Researchers should aim to be proactive and try as hard as possible at the planning stage to ensure that there are no practices in their research process that might harm participants. If there are any possible risks or harms, then these should be explained clearly. We will consider the importance of giving clear information about the research process in detail in Chapter 4. At this point it is useful to consider why people might be motivated to participate in a research project.

Reasons for participation

Participants have often spoken about their motivation for participating in our research and a wide range of reasons have been expressed. They may wish to share their experience and expertise for the benefit of others. It may contribute to their development by acting as a stimulus to think through their perspective on a particular topic. It may have a reparative function in that it could help them to understand more deeply how they feel about a particular issue or event. Participation may even be therapeutic in that it enables the person to tell their story and they feel better for having shared it with another person. It may also help them by knowing that their contribution may lead to service improvement, political action or legal changes; it can give them a voice that they may not otherwise have had. They may have a sense of duty to participate knowing that their contribution will be valuable, but also being aware that they may find the process painful. It may simply be a way to reduce feelings of isolation or assuage loneliness. Some of the reasons that participants gave for participating in one particular study are given in Box 2.4.

BOX 2.4   PARTICIPANTS' REASONS FOR PARTICIPATION

As part of his research on spirituality in psychoanalysis, Alistair interviewed a number of psychoanalysts, asking the question: 'Why were you willing to be interviewed?' There were a variety of answers. One person said 'I like being interviewed because it enables me to discover what I think'. Another said 'Nobody has ever asked me before and I felt I had something to say'. Yet another said 'I feel I owe it to you and to a new generation of thinkers to pass on something important'.

People may agree to participate because they find refusal difficult, they are in a powerless position, or they feel beholden to the researcher in some way. This is why it is usually considered to be good practice to have no prior connection with research participants. If there is a pre-existing relationship – as, for example, a friend, a fellow student, or a colleague – it may be hard for them to refuse because they fear it will impact negatively on the existing relationship. By pausing to think about why participants may have agreed to participate we can sensitise ourselves to these more subtle forms of participant vulnerability.

People in vulnerable situations

Participants' vulnerability may be dependent on their circumstances as they may live or work in a situation that places them at risk. While generally research should maximise the benefits for participants and minimise harm, it is possible that research could create or enhance this kind of vulnerability. For example, interviewing prisoners could be seen by other prisoners as colluding with authority and expose them to negative reactions. If a person prone to violence is aware that their partner is talking to a researcher about domestic violence, then the participant may be exposed to further risk. This kind of vulnerability can vary from day to day. Fontes (2004) warns that interviewing a woman whose partner is violent may be completely without risk on one particular day but result in serious injury or worse to the participant and the researcher at another time. Researcher awareness of the wider implications of participation for people can ensure extra care is taken in strengthening safeguards in relation to anonymity and ensuring that interviews take place in safe, discreet locations.

Sometimes it is clear that participants are in a less powerful position in relation to the researcher, for example, by virtue of being a student, an employee of an organisation, a prisoner, a refugee, a patient, a person in a psychiatric ward on a section, or any member of a less powerful group. In these situations it is important to ensure that any forms of pressure or coercion to participate in research are not present. Their powerlessness may mean that they are not always in a position to voice objection, so it may not be possible for them to give unfettered consent. These participants might believe a refusal to participate would impact on them negatively. Great care needs to be taken in the design and conduct of research to maximise the opportunities to refuse to take part and to ensure that refusal does not impact negatively on them. If authorisation and access to identified participants is obtained through third parties, such as organisations or institutions, there cannot be an assumption of consent by the individual concerned; this has to be individually obtained. Jemma Chambers did her doctoral research in a prison setting and in Box 2.5 she writes about the ethical dilemmas surrounding gaining informed consent from her participants.

BOX 2.5   GAINING INFORMED CONSENT FROM PRISONERS

My research was aimed at establishing the pathway that leads to a person committing a very serious assault (Chambers et al., 2009, 2011). It involved interviewing prisoners and the data was analysed by grounded theory and validated using Smallest Space Analysis

(Continued)

(Continued)

and Chi-square analysis. Ethical approval from a university and the Justice Departments was obtained, and plain language statements explaining the study, consent forms and debriefing statements were drafted for potential participants.

Participants were invited to take part in an interview, which lasted between a half and one and a half hours, about their childhood background, including their experience of violence and how it impacted upon the development of their attitudes. It also involved gathering detailed information about the violent/assault offence that they had committed, the time leading up to it, the offence itself and the time afterwards. The Justice Departments provided lists of prisoners who had convictions that aligned with the study inclusion criteria. Prisoners were then approached on their unit and they were invited to be told about the study, and then participated if they agreed. Participants also consented to access to their prison records so that I could collate information about their conviction history.

Theoretically, several areas of ethical importance were included in the plain-language statement, consent form and debriefing statement:

- Voluntary participation and the right to withdraw participation and the resulting data at any time before the study is written up.
- Information about what participation involves, including making clear that they would be talking about potentially distressing areas of life. Information about referral to third parties if distress occurs, for example, to a therapist unconnected to the study and prison.
- Anonymity: clarity that data recording using a tape player would occur; that the recordings would be destroyed after being transcribed, with the transcript being numbered only with an identification number and their name being kept separately. All data being kept securely and locked up with only the researcher having access. Publication of the thesis and journal articles will only contain aggregate data, and assurance that no one will be able to identify an individual prisoner.
- Informed consent: signing a consent form along with a witness – usually a member of prison staff.
- Collection of additional data from Department of Justice files.
- Bounds of confidentiality: making clear that we would only be speaking about an offence that the target conviction was for and if information comes to light about other offences the relevant authorities will be told.
- Avenues for further questions: contact details were provided of the official prison visitor, or complaints procedure, the principal researcher, the supervisor of the student, or the secretary of the ethics committee of the Department of Justice or for the university ethics committee.
- It was underlined that the project would not be of direct benefit to the prisoner.

The largest area of ethical practice for consideration from my experience of gathering data from prisoners was their autonomy. On paper the necessary steps were taken to ensure autonomy in participation in the study, such as making sure the participants understood what the study involved, gaining informed consent, explicitly outlining voluntary participation and the right to withdraw from participation and any data collected at any time before write-up (which allowed at least six months).

However, in practice these guidelines did not consider the system within which the participants existed. Although no direct benefit from the study was outlined, it may be important to consider what participants would gain from participating. I hypothesised that a reason why many individuals participated was to have the opportunity to talk to someone outside the prison system as their day-to-day contact was with other prisoners and justice system staff. I was a young woman in my mid-20s. Several of the participants stated that they had never told anyone in such detail about what had happened during their offence – we may assume that they had pleaded guilty in court, or that such detail was not required. There may be positive and negative consequences of this. First, they may have felt listened to and understood, which can be powerful in itself. Going over what was sometimes a distressing time in the participant's life may have brought suppressed feelings to consciousness, thus meaning that they required further help to process what had happened to them. Only one participant out of the 48 interviewed became visibly distressed when recounting their story; the rest often spoke in an emotionally detached manner, which may be assumed was a defence for the lifetime of abuse that the majority of participants described. However, no participants contacted me for additional support or therapeutic intervention following the study. I would hypothesise that this was due to the participants' defences, which were already in place, and that rupture of these defences would require significant challenging and in-depth analysis, neither of which were present in the interview.

Overall, the study provided valuable information about the pathways that lead up to people committing violent offences. In particular, it highlighted histories of childhood abuse and deprivation. My hope is that any distress that I caused to prisoners will be balanced by providing evidence that indicates that greater care and support given to children in abusive and deprived situations can have long-term positive effects for society as a whole.

Jemma C. Chambers

The issue of participant vulnerability

Most people have their vulnerabilities and, from this perspective, we can regard all participants as potentially vulnerable. However, it is clear that some prospective participants will have pre-existing vulnerabilities that require special forethought and care. This may be due to a physical or psychological condition, or they may have been subjected to some form of trauma, deprivation or marginalisation that affects their decision-making abilities. A broad definition of this kind of vulnerable research participant is anyone who does not have the capacity to give informed consent and/or who may be harmed by some aspect of the research process. The harm may be physical, psychological, emotional or reputational damage.

The researcher's responsibility towards participants calls for sensitivity to any form of participant vulnerability. However, the issue of vulnerability is itself problematic and subjective. Individuals who may come to mind as belonging to a vulnerable group might well find this classification patronising and even consider it to be an insidious form of paternalism that prevents their voices from being heard. For example, Barnes (2009) highlights the social construction of disability, where historically disability has been seen in terms of deficit and individual pathology. The social model of disability draws attention to the fact that people with impairments are disabled by environmental and cultural barriers, rather than by any personal factors. By defining people as, for example, disabled, and therefore vulnerable, they can be excluded from engagement in research or have their contribution attenuated. The emancipatory research tradition (Zarb, 1992) has highlighted this form of exclusion and argues for the inclusion of participants at every stage of the research process in order to ensure that decisions are not being made about the research process that might lead to the marginalisation of people who are positioned as vulnerable.

However, the term 'vulnerable participants' does appear on some ethics forms and in ethics guidelines. It is also used to highlight the possibility of harm and increased risks to participants when researching particular populations (Lott, 2005). People from the following groups are often described as vulnerable participants. First, there are people who have a reduced capacity to participate fully in decision making. This category can include children, young people, and people with learning difficulties or forms of cognitive impairment such as dementia. Secondly, due to temporary factors such as physical or mental illness, people may have a limited ability to make reasoned decisions or may not be in a position to voice objections and so it is not possible for them to give informed or freely given consent. Deciding who might be vulnerable is not a simple matter. For example, there has been a tendency for ethics committee members to underestimate the ability of psychiatric in-patients to give informed consent and to overestimate the capacity of people who have physical illnesses (Luebbert et al., 2008). Further evidence for the over-estimation of the capacities of people with physical illness was found by Raymont et al. (2004), who discovered that up to 40 per cent of hospital in-patients suffering from physical illnesses may have a diminished ability to make decisions.

When considering involving people who may have a reduced ability to make decisions, the primary criterion is that the research study being undertaken should contribute to the well-being of participants. The secondary criterion is that the participation of these particular participants is necessary because the data cannot be obtained by any other means. The possible impact of research participation for them at that time and at future times should be considered and the research methodology and process should be appropriate and ensure their physical and psychological safety. The additional consent of parents or a proxy such as a carer, medical staff, an advocate, or social worker, should be sought in these circumstances. If there are two parents, then both should be involved in the permission procedure. At times the carers may be enthusiastic for the research to take place, so it is also very important that sensitivity to the needs of the participant is prioritised. The consent of the proxy should not be regarded as a replacement for the consent of the participant.

As well as the carer's consent the participant should also be asked for their consent and the project should be carefully explained to them in a way that maximises the possibility for understanding. It is often helpful for the researcher to have established some form of prior contact with the participant so that the researcher is not a stranger and the participant feels able to express themselves in their presence. Wilson and Powell (2001) underline the importance of attending to the environment where the research is to take place and suggest comfortable surroundings with seating arrangements that minimise any feeling of disparity in power relations. It may be helpful to use a variety of media to aid communication, such as visual representations. Cameron (2005) provides a helpful guide for researchers working with children. She discusses the usefulness of a variety of communication methods to facilitate the development of an effective research relationship and to aid in gathering data. The methods reviewed include free-narrative, puppets, drawing, painting and modelling. Some of these methods may be usefully adapted to aid communication with adult participants. However, some caution has to be exercised in the interpretation of these projective techniques. Although a drawing can be useful as a basis for discussion, it is not always easy to discern accurately what the participant may have intended to convey.

Establishing a set of ground rules at the beginning of the contact can help to reduce anxiety by defining the boundaries of the encounter and acting as a guide to expectations about the research process. Ground rules can include things such as what the researcher and participant would like to be called and how the participant can 'manage' the interaction by agreeing how they can signal that they do not want to engage with particular aspects of the research, such as answering specific questions or doing certain activities (Wilson and Powell, 2001).

The most productive starting point when embarking on research is to see participants first as people and not solely through the lens of any vulnerability. A more apt approach is to consider what are their abilities? How can their participation in this research be ethically facilitated? Christensen and Prout (2002) argue for the establishment of ethical symmetry. They developed this concept in relation to research with children, but it can be applied equally to all people who might be regarded as 'vulnerable'. They describe ethical symmetry in the following way:

> By this we mean that the researcher takes as his or her starting point the view that the ethical relationship between researcher and informant is the same whether he or she conducts research with adults or with children. This has a number of implications. The first is that the researcher employs the same ethical principles whether they are researching children or adults. Second, that each right and ethical consideration in relation to adults in the research process has its counterpart for children. Third, the symmetrical treatment of children in research means that any differences between carrying out research with children or with adults should be allowed to arise from this starting point, according to the concrete situation of children, rather than being assumed in advance.

(Christensen and Prout, 2002: 482)

Ethical symmetry is achieved by conducting a continuous dialogue with participants throughout the research process. It is only through this careful process of discussion and consultation that the unique abilities and needs of 'potentially vulnerable' participants can be kept in the foreground of practice. Christensen and Prout (2002) emphasise the value of an interplay of codes of ethics, researcher reflexivity and collective professional responsibility. Codes provide useful structure and guidance. Researcher reflexivity enables moment-by-moment ethical decisions to be taken and embraces the need for the flexibility that particular situations may demand. Collective professional responsibility is achieved through the maintenance of an open dialogue with research colleagues, which enables the ethical values and principles that underpin the research to be continuously debated and reviewed.

While verbal consent may be given by vulnerable participants, the researcher needs to be alert moment by moment to signs of distress, discomfort or any indication that the person no longer wishes to participate. This level of care should be taken throughout each stage of the research study. Vulnerable participants' capacity to understand the implications of participation may differ at various points in time and be dependent on external factors, such as who is present and where the research is conducted. Instead of assuming a limited capacity to participate, researchers should focus on establishing a research relationship that complements and supports the decision-making capacities of vulnerable people. Essentially, an adequate assessment of participant ability involves setting aside generalised views on the abilities of particular client groups and assessing the specific abilities of each individual in the context of their particular circumstances.

Disclosures or observations that identify vulnerability

Occasionally, during a research project it may become apparent that the participant is in a situation that involves significant risk, such as some form of abuse involving serious harm to the participant or other person. This might be, for example, a disclosure of child abuse or the researcher observing harmful institutional practices while conducting the research. It is important at the planning stage to consider the likelihood of such disclosures or observations being made. Being aware that this possibility may arise, the researcher can then ensure that they have arrangements in place for dealing with such an instance. Prior planning can include consultation with representatives and professionals involved with the particular group and gaining knowledge of the procedures to be followed if such a disclosure or observation is made. It is also necessary to be transparent about the actions that may be taken in the initial information given to participants so that they are aware of what may happen if they make such disclosures. If institutional failure is uncovered, it should be fed back to the organisation in the best way possible to ensure that appropriate action is taken. Effective supervisory support is invaluable in these situations.

The vulnerability of third parties

It is also necessary to consider if the conduct of the research or its dissemination will impact negatively on any third parties. This could be an individual, family members, a group of people, an organisation, or the wider community. In the example given in Box 2.6, it is clear that the researcher had not thought through the complications that can arise when interviewing participants in their own homes.

BOX 2.6 AN UNANTICIPATED IMPACT

During a research study on work stress participants were given a choice of interview location. For reasons of confidentiality, one man asked to be interviewed at home on a Saturday morning. The interview was going well. We had exceeded the agreed one hour but the participant wanted to carry on as he felt that there was a good deal more to say on the emotionally-laden topic of the research. As we continued, I became aware of doors banging and the noise of people stomping around outside the room. I mentioned this to the participant and he said that it was his wife and children. He had forgotten about our interview until a short while before I arrived and had previously promised to take them out that morning. He went on to say that he supposed that his wife might also be cross because he had always refused to talk to her about his work. It helped him to keep his work and home lives separate but she had never been happy about it. It was clear that my presence was upsetting for his wife and it was likely that the interview was going to be the cause of marital discord. The family had also had their Saturday morning outing spoilt. I had not thought in any depth about the impact of home interviews on the other members of the household before. I was much more careful about it after this experience.

What is a sensitive research topic?

Allied to participant vulnerability is the potential sensitivity of the research topic. A sensitive topic is any subject that may expose participants or third parties to significant harm, or evoke distress or feelings of disturbance. While the potentially sensitive nature of some topics may be obvious, and it is clear that safeguards need to be in place, there may be highly individual risks or sensitivities that are difficult to anticipate. This calls for the researcher to maintain awareness of the impact that the research may be having on their participants. For example, a loss may be evoked and the impact of grief should never be underestimated, no matter how much time has elapsed. If a painful memory is re-stimulated, it is not necessary to shut down the interview or area of enquiry. Provide support for the participant so that they can make their own choice about whether to end the interview and, if they wish to continue, respect their feelings by giving them space to tell their story. A key to avoid evoking unanticipated distress is to ensure that the participants are fully aware of the nature of the research. Sensitive subjects should not be avoided as research topics, but extra care is needed in the planning and process of the projects to ensure that the wider implications of the research process and possible risks are thought through.

One essential aspect of planning is the choice of an appropriate research methodology. Attempting to explore a sensitive subject with a 'distancing' methodology may increase participant distress. So exploring a very sensitive subject by questionnaire may cause distress, but similar questions asked by a researcher during an interview can have a less negative impact as they can be modified or developed according to the emotions expressed by the participant. Structuring the interview so that it leads up progressively to the more delicate questions, checking that the participant is happy to continue, and emphasising the right to refuse to answer questions or terminate the interview can ensure that unnecessary distress is avoided. On the other hand, people may be more comfortable about disclosing sensitive information via an anonymous questionnaire. A less intrusive form of contact may be preferred when there is the possibility of shame being related to the topic, for example, in research into sexual behaviour.

Conclusion

The aim of this chapter is to focus researchers' thinking on their participants and to gain a heightened awareness of their responsibilities in relation to their participants. An understanding of the controversy that surrounds the designation of participants as vulnerable and focusing on the capacities of individuals rather than viewing identified groups of people as vulnerable enables more appropriate ethical judgements to be made. The ability to decentre and view the world from the perspective of the participant enhances sensitive decision making.

There is probably no greater means for researchers to sensitise themselves to the nuances of being a participant than by volunteering to be a participant themselves. Most undergraduate psychology courses require students to be research participants; it is less common in counselling, nursing and social work training. It is often only when we put ourselves in a particular situation that we can begin to understand what it really involves. From thinking about research from the position of participants, it becomes clear that the success of research is closely related to the quality of the relationships that we establish with them. The development and maintenance of the research relationship is the subject of the next chapter.

REFLECTIVE QUESTIONS

- How do you respond to Levinas's idea that we are 'captive' to 'the face of the other'?
- What degree of responsibility should be taken in relation to the people involved in your research?
- If you were asked to take part in a research project, what would be your motivation for participating?
- How useful is the concept of vulnerability in relation to participation?
- Which alternative forms of communication could you usefully use to explain your research study to participants?
- What do you consider would be a sensitive topic for you as a research participant and how would you like the research to be approached?

References

Annas, G.J. and Grodin, M.A. (2008). The Nuremberg Code. In E.J. Emanuel, C. Grady, R.A. Crouch, R.K. Lie, F.G. Miller and D. Wendler (Eds.), *The Oxford Textbook of Clinical Research Ethics*. Oxford: Oxford University Press.

Ashcroft, R.E. (2008). The Declaration of Helsinki. In E.J. Emanuel, C. Grady, R.A. Crouch, R.K. Lie, F.G. Miller and D. Wendler (Eds.), *The Oxford Textbook of Clinical Research Ethics*. Oxford: Oxford University Press.

Barnes, C. (2009). An ethical agenda in disability research: rhetoric or reality? In D. M. Mertens and P.E. Ginsberg (Eds.), *The Handbook of Social Research Ethics*. London: Sage.

Bauman, Z. (1993). *Postmodern Ethics*. Oxford: Blackwell.

Cameron, H. (2005). Asking tough questions: a guide to ethical practices in interviewing young children. *Early Child Development and Care*, 175(6): 597–610.

Chambers, J.C., Ward, T., Eccleston, L. and Brown, M. (2009). The Pathways Model of Assault: a qualitative analysis of the assault offender and offence. *Journal of Interpersonal Violence*, 24: 1423–1449.

Chambers, J.C., Ward, T., Eccleston, L. and Brown, M. (2011). Representation of female offender types within the Pathways Model of Assault. *International Journal of Offender Therapy and Comparative Criminology*, 55: 925–948.

Christensen, P. and Prout, A. (2002). Working with ethical symmetry in social research with children. *Childhood*, 9: 477–497.

Dona, G. (2007). The microphysics of participation in refugee research. *Journal of Refugee Studies*, 20(2): 210–229.

Fontes, L.A. (2004). Ethics in violence against women research: the sensitive, the dangerous, and the overlooked. *Ethics and Behavior*, 14(2): 141–174.

Fromm, E. (1973). *The Anatomy of Human Destructiveness*. St Paul, MN: Fawcett Crest Books.

Gordon, P. (1999). *Face to Face: Therapy as Ethics*. London: Constable.

Grossman, V. (2006). *Life and Fate*. Trans. R. Chandler. London: Vintage.

Levinas, E. (1990 [1963]). *Difficult Freedom: Essays on Judaism*. Trans S. Hand. Baltimore, MD: Johns Hopkins University Press.

Lott, J.P. (2005). Module Three: vulnerable/special participant populations. *Developing World Bioethics*, 5(1): 30–54.

Luebbert, R., Tait, R.C., Chibnall, J.T. and Deshields, T.L. (2008). Institutional review board member judgements of decisional capacity, coercion, and risk in medical and psychiatric studies. *Journal of Empirical Research on Human Research Ethics*, 3(1): 15–24.

Lurie, P. and Wolfe, S.M. (1997). Unethical trials of interventions to reduce perinatal transmission of the human immunodeficiency virus in developing countries. *New England Journal of Medicine*, 337: 853–856.

Milgram, S. (1974). *Obedience to Authority: An Experimental View*. London: Tavistock.

Oliver, M. (1997). Emancipatory research: realistic goal or impossible dream. In C. Barnes and G. Mercer (Eds.), *Doing Disability Research*. Leeds: The Disability Press.

Orange, D.M. (2010). *Thinking for Clinicians: Philosophical Resources for Contemporary Psychoanalysis and the Humanistic Psychotherapies*. New York: Routledge.

Parker, I. (2000). Obedience. *Granta*, 71: 99–125.

Raymont, V., Bingley, W., Buchanan, A., David, A.S., Hayward, P., Wessely, S. and Hotopf, M. (2004). Prevalence of mental capacity in medical inpatients and associated risk factors: cross-sectional study. *Lancet*, 364: 1421–1427.

Robbins, J. (Ed.) (2001). *Is it Righteous to Be? Interviews with Emmanuel Levinas*. Stanford, CA: Stanford University Press.

The Nuremberg Code (1947). Accessed on 29 April 2012 at http://ohsr.od.nih.gov/guidelines/nuremberg.html

US Holocaust Memorial Museum (2012). Accessed on 28 April 2012 at www.ushmm.org/wlc/en/article.php?ModuleId=10005250

Wilson, C. and Powell, M. (2001). *A Guide to Interviewing Children: Essential Skills for Counsellors, Police, Lawyers and Social Workers*. Sydney, NSW: Allen & Unwin.

World Medical Association (1964). *Code of Ethics of the World Medical Association: Declaration of Helsinki*. Helsinki, Finland: WMA.

World Medical Association. (2008). *Declaration of Helsinki* (8th amendment). Accessed on 29 April 2012 at www.wma.net/en/30publications/10policies/b3/index.html

Wright, T., Hughes, P. and Ainley, A. (1988). The paradox of morality: an interview with Emmanuel Levinas. In R. Bernasconi and D. Wood (Eds.), *The Provocation of Levinas*. London: Routledge.

Zarb, G. (1992). On the road to Damascus: first steps towards changing the relations of disability research production. *Disability, Handicap and Society*, 7(2): 125–138.

Zimbardo, P.G. (1973). On the ethics of intervention in human psychological research: with special reference to the Stanford Prison Experiment. *Cognition*, 2: 243–256.

3

Relational ethics: the relationship between the researcher and the participant

Research has shown that the quality of the relationship between therapist and client is one of the most important factors in a successful outcome in counselling and psychotherapy. This applies equally to nursing and social work relationships (Noddings, 1984; Ruch et al., 2010). The relationship has also been a focus of attention for philosophers and researchers alike. Even if a researcher never actually meets their participant, a relationship still exists and has to be maintained. For all forms of research, we would argue, the relationship is of pivotal importance. This chapter begins by focusing on relational ethics which informs our thinking about the research relationship. We then look more closely at the factors that contribute to the formation and maintenance of research relationships.

Relational ethics has emerged as a distinct category of ethics in the last twenty-five years. Yet what sort of ethics is it? Is it an application of existing ethical thinking? Is it a form of virtue ethics expressed in the relational language of the late twentieth and early twenty-first centuries? Is it a universalistic ethic, and, if so, how might it engage with concrete situations? The answers to these questions may be found in its origins but, even if they are not, it is always important to know where we have come from in order to understand the current situation. There are a number of interwoven strands that form the contemporary tapestry of relational ethics. These are: a focus on an ethics of care; the emergence of postmodernism; the expansion of qualitative research methodologies; developments in professional identity and expertise; the concept of the wounded healer; and the rediscovery of relational philosophy.

A focus on an ethics of care

In the 1970s the feminist philosopher Carol Gilligan (1982) advocated an 'ethic of care' based on her original critique that women and men deal with ethical questions differently. Women adopt a 'relational' stance deriving from an ethics of care, and men adopt a 'rational' stance deriving from an ethics of justice. Her work has seen elaboration, modi-fication and critique (Allmark, 1995; Baier, 1985; Held, 1993, 2006; Noddings, 1984, 2002) as it is rather simplistic to polarise gender in this way, yet it sparked a produc-tive debate, as justice and care are equally important. This development was immensely valuable in enabling ethicists to think about the social, political and cultural contexts of ethics and the nature of power. Gilligan helpfully brought together notions of eth-ics, care and the relational, which have become vital components of the emerging field of relational ethics. Nel Noddings has further developed an ethics of care focused on the importance of relationships in education and wider social contexts. Gilligan's (1982; Gilligan et al., 1988) and Noddings' (1984, 2002) work has contributed to a feminist relational ethics that sees all research as value-laden and linked with an implicit culture. As such relational ethics offers a form of reflexive engagement to discern what is of value above and beyond the limitations of cultural and gendered norms (Priessle, 2007).

The emergence of postmodernism

The rise of postmodernism has challenged the existence of absolute truths. Modernism posited that it was possible to find overarching explanations (metanarratives) for phe-nomena. The postmodern position is that truth is relative and contextual. If we adopt 'incredulity towards metanarratives' (Lyotard, 1984), these metanarratives have been replaced by local and situated relational narratives, in which ethics takes a more central position. Gadow (1999) sees the rise of relational narratives directly linked to the post-modern turn in nursing ethics. She summarises her ideas thus:

> A philosophy of nursing requires an ethical cornerstone. I describe three dialectical layers of an ethical cornerstone: subjective immersion, objective detachment, and relational nar-rative. Dialectically, the move from immersion to detachment is the turn from communi-tarian to rational ethics, replacing traditions with universal principles. The move from universalism to engagement is the turn from rational to relational ethics, replacing detached reason with engagement between particular selves. Conceptually, the three lay-ers correspond to pre-modern, modern, and postmodern ethics. I propose that the layers be viewed not as stages, but as elements that coexist in an ethically vital profession.

(Gadow, 1999: 57)

The expansion of qualitative research methods

Postmodern thought and the increasing acceptance of multiple narratives has led to the wider recognition of and use of qualitative methodologies. The development of qualita-tive research, not just as an alternative to quantitative research, but as systems of thought that challenge assumptions and focus on the location of the researcher and the participant, has found an ally in relational ethics (Denzin and Lincoln, 2011). Relational ethics have developed alongside the fields of ethnography and autoethnography, and autoethnographic approaches have been very effectively used in a wide range of studies and disciplines (Ward, 2012). Ward argues that ethnography has several foundational principles, including the adoption of an 'active participative ethic', which require an 'ethical commitment', though he stops short of saying what these might be (Ward, 2012: 6–7). Ellis (2007; Ellis et al., 2011) has been pursuing the vital importance of such approaches for the last twenty years, while Etherington (2004), writing as a feminist thinker and therapist in the area of autoethnography, posits that we can become reflexive researchers who use our selves in research.

These changes in research practice raised new issues about research ethics, validity and representation, and the purpose of undertaking research (Josselson, 1996). Such research enabled the voices of people who had previously been marginalised and oppressed to be heard. Research can therefore be used to effect changes in society and to challenge oppressive and unhealthy practices. So we come to relational ethics not just as a matter of academic interest. We come as researchers engaging in relationships with others that have the power either to maintain the status quo or to change the way people see themselves and the wider context of their lives.

Developments in professional identity and expertise

An example of how people and professions can change has been seen in the emergence of nursing as a profession in search of a unique identity and areas of expertise. Gadow's ideas have proved influential and been picked up by others advancing relational ethics in the field of nursing (Hess, 2003). Particular attention has been paid to relational ethics by the nursing profession in Canada. In 1993 the Social Sciences and Humanities Research Council of Canada funded an interdisciplinary group of healthcare professionals and academics to research relational ethics and ethical relationships. Adopting concepts of engaged interaction, mutual respect, embodied knowledge, uncertainty or vulnerability, freedom and choice, and the significance of the environment, this work was published as *Relational Ethics: The Full Meaning of Respect* (Bergum and Dossetor, 2005). While the project finished in 2000, it provided the context for the establishment of the Canada Research Chair in Relational Ethics in Health Care. Further work on relational ethics has led to it being viewed as an action-based process grounded in everyday health situations, expanding to include engagement, dialogue, presence (Evans et al., 2004) and, more recently, advocacy (MacDonald, 2007).

The 'relational turn' is a term that has been used to describe how counselling, psychotherapy and psychoanalysis have changed in the last two decades. An emphasis on the fundamental importance of the ethical basis of the therapeutic relationship to counselling and psychotherapy practice is to be found in the work of Gordon (1999) and Loewenthal and Snell (2003). Gordon (1999) offers a perspective of therapy as ethics and argues that in the face-to-face encounter we both change and are changed by our clients. Levinas figures significantly in this approach, but how are the relational and ethical configured in this therapeutic context? Gabriel and Casemore (2009) offer a broad perspective combining subjectivity and inter-subjectivity (though they do not use these terms). We can construe relational ethics as a co-constructed ethical and moral encounter, with associated relationship experiences and processes, which both influences and in turn is influenced by the complex multidimensional context in which relationship occurs. The term 'relational ethic' represents the complex medium through which decisions and interactions associated with the processes and progress of a relationship are mindfully and ethically engaged with (Gabriel and Casemore, 2009: 1). Gabriel and Casemore (2009) argue that all therapeutic relationships involve ethical encounters, but the character of those encounters varies enormously and differs from the very prescriptive forms of ethics or ethical codes that have been shaped by a knowing and authoritative stance.

The concept of the wounded healer

There has been a considerable amount written on the phenomenon of the wounded healer (Conti-O'Hare, 2002; Goldberg, 1986; Hennessey, 2011; Jackson, 2001; Nouwen, 1979; Tillett, 2003; Wheeler, 2007). This literature and its allied research focus on the unconscious motivations of people who enter the caring professions. For some, the desire to care for other people results from the high quality of their early nurturing, and this creates a natural impulse to pass it on to others. For others, there is a significant failing in early relationships that is compensated for by seeking positive relationships through service to others. Alternatively, there may be a formative early experience, such as an experience of trauma, serious illness or observation of the illness or death of another, that has sensitised the child to the needs of people in these situations. The work on the motivations of 'healers' has focused thinking on the dynamics of relationships within the caring professions and added to our understanding of professional relationships.

The rediscovery of relational philosophy

There has been a rediscovery of relational philosophers or philosophers focusing on relationality (Loewenthal and Snell, 2003; Zimmermann, 2007). Relational ethics builds on the premise that our understanding of ourselves is of a person in relationship. The philosopher, John Macmurray, writes:

> Persons, therefore, are constituted by their mutual relation to one another. 'I' exist only as one element in the complex 'You and I'. …. But within this relation, which constitutes my existence, I can isolate myself from you in intention, so that my relation to you becomes impersonal. In this event, I treat you as an object, refusing the personal relationship.

(Macmurray, 1961: 27–28)

Macmurray's ideas built on those of Buber (1958) and overlap with Levinas, in what Becker and Becker (2003) see as a new trend in continental philosophy. There emerged a new foundation for relational ethics, at the heart of which was a unique focus on persons in relation to each other.

Helpful insights into what makes a relationship can be found in the influential work of Martin Buber, a nineteenth-century Jewish existential philosopher and religious thinker (Buber, 1958). Buber, a near contemporary of Freud, was born in Vienna in 1878 and grew up with his grandparents in Poland. He was hugely influenced by a Hasidic form of Judaism. Hasidism emphasises practical and community spirituality, affirming each person in their wholeness, because in doing so one transforms the self and the world for God. Buber had early links with Zionism and from 1904 to 1938 taught Jewish religious studies and ethics at Frankfurt University (although he was banned from teaching from 1933 onwards). In 1938 he left Germany to become a professor at the Hebrew University, Jerusalem, teaching anthropology and sociology.

Buber became famous for his classic book, *Ich und Du* (later translated into English as *I and Thou* in 1925). He describes the ultimate state of being as one where there is a relational engagement with the natural world, other people (individually and collectively), and other spiritual realities. There are two basic forms of relating: the I–Thou and the I–It. The I–Thou is a mutual, reciprocal relation; the I–It is a passive subject–object relation; and both are located beyond the self. Buber's ideas have proved to be enduringly popular as they capture something that makes sense to us, although there is always the danger that we take these ideas too literally. These are not static or fixed polarities. Every Thou has the potential to become an It, while every I–It has the potential to become an I–Thou in a transforming encounter. In Buber's words, this 'intimate relationship … "I–Thou" can only be spoken with the whole being' (Buber, 1958: 15). In this relational event there is a meeting with what has been variously described as the absolute Other (echoes of Levinas), the eternal Thou, as 'this is the only I–Thou relation that can be sustained indefinitely, for God is wholly other' (Hand, 1989: 59). The One who is beyond the self would, in Christian terms, be described as God.

While Buber's writing has a mystical heritage, its influence in the twentieth century was acquired by being taken up by existential philosophers, theologians and therapists. What Buber does so well is to put relationship, as a central quality of relational being, at the heart of human existence. Buber's ideas are evocative and widely used, but always need to be treated with a little caution as he is so often taken out of context. It can be argued that while Buber recognises the other, the 'Thou', it is always in relation to the 'I', and there is a danger in research that the focus always comes back to the researcher. In Buber's terms, this would be an 'I–It' relationship, whereas in a relational ethic, one would be striving towards an 'I–Thou' experience that is shared between the researcher and the participant.

Orange (2010) offers an insightful analysis and application of Buber's ideas for therapists, but we use Buber here to underpin our view that the relationship between the researcher and the researched, while starting as an 'I–It' relationship, always has the potential to become so much more as an 'I–Thou' relationship. People in the caring professions want to make a difference to people and want to be involved relationally in order to achieve this. The relationship between the researcher and the participant is just as significant, so it is unsurprising that a whole field of study has evolved around the term 'relational ethics'.

Relational ethics in research practice

How do relational ethics influence the way we do research? They are especially important for research methodologies that privilege a direct relationship with participants. Being in the room with a person enhances the relational dimension and brings with it a number of important issues of which we need to be aware. Although some researchers may not directly encounter their participants, holding in mind a sense of an I–Thou relationship with the unseen participants can enhance ethical practice. Focusing on the relational dimension of research processes requires engaging in a delicate balancing act. We need to be sufficiently involved with the participants in order for a real meeting to take place that engages the 'other' (using Levinas's term) and which is more of an I–Thou relationship than an I–It relationship (using Buber's terms). Yet this must be balanced with the need to develop and maintain a degree of objectivity. Such critical reflexivity focuses on the research task of eliciting important information, ideas, thoughts and feelings. These contribute to the research agenda of developing new insights, forming the substance of the research in which we are engaged.

In the course of research, the following relational areas need attention and reflection: the relationship with the research context; the relationship with the research subject; building a research relationship; and maintaining a research relationship.

A relationship with the research context

If we believe an I–Thou relational engagement is important for our research, it is equally important that we recognise our location as a researcher. We can locate ourselves by asking a number of questions often raised under the subject of difference. How might I define myself in terms of age, gender, class, race and ethnicity, orientation, or ability? This list can be extended but the answers we find help clarify how we see ourselves and this may have a significant bearing in relation to the research we do. Such a reflective approach may identify that we have a pre-existing relationship to the research subject or participants that we might not have been aware of and is essential for effective research to take place. In the example in Box 3.1, we can see how a reflective awareness of the researcher's life-story influenced her ability to do effective research.

BOX 3.1   CONTEXTUAL FACTORS CAN FACILITATE THE RESEARCH RELATIONSHIP

As a result of her own childhood experience of domestic violence, Sue became a volunteer in a women's refuge offering listening and using counselling skills in an informal capacity. In selecting her research subject she decided to examine the women's experience of therapy in this context. Given the traumatic experience many of them had been

---

through and the real threat to their safety, Sue was very clear about the limits of disclo-sure and confidentiality. Some of the women volunteered not because Sue was their therapist, as she did not interview any of her clients, but because they knew her and trusted her. It was clear that she respected them and understood the complexities of their situations. They noted that she had been around for some time and had formed a good relationship with them because she was interested in them as people, and not just as research subjects. Sue was seen as a point of safe anchorage and not like some of the other professionals they had encountered who seemed to change with great rapidity.

A relationship with the research subject

As mentioned in Chapter 1, researchers often choose a specific subject that is of personal interest without realising that this can have major consequences and complications. We return to this important theme, focusing on how our personal history might influence or make an impact on our relationship with research participants. While not everyone accepts the validity of the concept of unconscious processes, if they do exist, it means that our unconscious history is available to the unconscious of the research participant and has the potential to make an impression, good or bad. Etherington (2004: 209) sees that even being aware of our own biases may not 'sufficiently guard us from their allure' or their influence on our participants. We need to be alert to the possibility of being caught up in a complex dynamic that links with our personal history. This is especially true in areas such as abuse and trauma where there is a danger of unconsciously repeat-ing an abusive or traumatic pattern. The example in Box 3.2 describes how these factors led to a student nearly failing his Master's degree.

BOX 3.2   ETHICAL OVER-ENGAGEMENT

Gordon was a social work student doing a Master's degree. Before training he had a traumatic experience and this influenced his decision to study the lived experience of trauma in clients. His academic supervisors suggested another subject but Gordon was adamant this was the area he wanted to research. Gordon did eight interviews but he began to experience overwhelming emotions and flashbacks. His investigation had re-traumatised him and at times he was unable to distinguish between his research participants' traumas and his own. This created a dynamic in the research relationship of ethical over-engagement, and Gordon became convinced that he must represent everything his participants had said. This made writing-up extremely stressful. Gordon needed extra time and a good deal of support from his supervisor and the university counselling service in order to complete his degree.

Good research is often 'experience near' (Hollway, 2009), but the degree of engagement should not overwhelm the research process. In the following example (Box 3.3), the researcher raised her awareness of the powerful personal emotions that might arise during her study and this enabled her to produce a richer, well-balanced analysis.

BOX 3.3   UNCONSCIOUS IMPOSITIONS

When one lone twin, whose twin died at birth, wanted to examine this subject for a thesis her supervisor helped her see that her associations were very powerful in relation to this aspect of herself that she could not easily access. She did examine this area by interviewing other lone twins but needed careful supervision to avoid her own conscious and unconscious impositions on the research. These insights were captured as an important part of her research experience in a reflexive section of her thesis (Hayton, 2009).

Hayton's (2009) reflexive account is an example of 'conscious partiality' (Mies, 1983: 123). Olesen (2005: 255) describes conscious partiality as the creation of 'a critical conceptual distance between the researcher and the participants dialectically to facilitate correction of distortions on both sides'. Clearly, identification of and engagement with the other is important, but not at the cost of merging or over-identifying with the participant (Etherington, 2004).

This also raises the complex issue of self-disclosure. Oakley (1981) advocates answering the questions her research participants raised as a form of equality and respect, but she did not volunteer personal information. Relational ethics offers a balance between being real with the participants in a way that is alert to power dynamics and imbalances, unconscious processes, and the all-pervasive ethical responsibility for the other, while offering a reciprocal respect for their human experience. At the beginning of the research process we offer information about ourselves, usually through an information sheet, but we need to think about what this contains and how this might enhance or hinder the process. Our reason for engaging with 'the other' is in order to do research that respects their contribution, advances a cause, advocates change or enables new insights to emerge, yet the reason for establishing this relationship is on the basis of a research focus. This clarity needs to be kept in mind at the same time as we engage in a real relationship. An example of appropriate self-disclosure is given in Box 3.4.

BOX 3.4   ESTABLISHING A REAL RELATIONSHIP

When researching spirituality and psychoanalysis, I chose to reveal to participants that I was a minister of religion. Not all the potential research participants I approached agreed to be interviewed, and so I did not know if this information was unhelpful and prevented their participation. I felt that it made more sense to place my research and myself in a context, while adopting an open enquiring stance on issues of spirituality informed by my theological background. Several research participants were as keen to hear from me as I was to hear from them. One, who self-identified as an atheist, asked

---

> which theologians I read. He found this helpful as it balanced what at times felt like an unbalanced power dynamic.

Oakley advises:

> Ethical dilemmas are generic to all research involving interviews … but they are greatest when there is least social distance between the interviewer and the interviewee. Where both share the same gender socialisation and critical life-experiences, social distance can be minimal. Where both … share membership of the same minority group, the basis for equality may impress itself even more urgently on the interviewer's consciousness.

(Oakley, 1981: 55)

Building a research relationship

People in the counselling, nursing and social work professions who work therapeutically will be familiar with the concept of a working alliance based on the work of Bordin (1979, 1980, 1983, 1994) and further developed by Castonguay et al. (2006). Bordin identified three components of the alliance between a client and a therapist that were predictors of good therapeutic outcomes (Horvath and Symonds, 1991; Martin et al., 2000). These were a focus on agreed goals, specific tasks and an emotional bond. Gabriel and Casemore (2009) adapt Bordin's ideas and apply them to the research alliance, where the goal becomes the research aims, the task becomes the research processes (such as a semi-structured interview), and the bond becomes the relationship between researcher and participant. New researchers often focus on the goals and tasks of research – the more 'mechanical' aspect of research. This involves: recruiting suitable participants (a major task in its own right); agreeing a time and place for an interview; travelling to the venue; using recording equipment; gaining specific consent (often in the form of a signed letter); and transcribing the material in preparation for some form of analysis. While these aspects are important, the research alliance is a relationship that needs to be built and maintained in order to enhance the research relationship.

Maintaining the research relationship

People new to research may be unprepared for the complexity of the feelings that can be generated through a relational research process. As we engage in research, we need to be aware that the encounters can be powerful, enlightening, moving, disappointing, painful or just difficult. The dynamics that evolve can be unpredictable and take unexpected directions. Just as the participants have an impact on us, we may also have an impact on them (as can be seen in the example in Box 3.5) and it can cause unexpected dilemmas.

> ### BOX 3.5   THE SOCIAL MEETING DILEMMA
>
> In one interview the person disclosed some personal information because the interview had gone so well and the interviewee felt they could trust me. In subsequent contact, elicited by follow-up questions raised by the research, they suggested a social meeting – going to the theatre when I was next in their city. It felt important to me to maintain a professional relationship, as the means of my getting to know them arose out of a research relationship. It was a reminder to me of the feelings that can arise through engaging in a research process where we are asking people to reveal aspects of their personal and professional lives.

If only it were as simple as has been outlined above, as the professional relationship cannot be something that we can hide behind as a means of protection. It would be better to be aware that in relational ethics viewing the 'other' as vitally important has consequences. In counselling or therapeutic contexts, where a depth of engagement between client and therapist is commonplace, this is managed through practice supervision. The complexities that arise in the research relationship raise questions as to whether the nature of supervision in a research process needs to be able to encompass more than just the academic dimension.

When establishing research relationships, we must also be aware that we bring to this a wide experience of people skills. Counsellors, social workers and nurses have roles that combine a range of technical, theoretical, practical and relational skills, that make a profound difference to the people we are researching. To be thought of and treated as a person rather than a patient or client means a great deal and affirms a person's unique sense of self. Consequently, most good practitioners have developed a wide range of skills, and are especially effective listeners, even if they have not had any formal counselling training. These skills include listening at a number of different levels. People tell us things if they see we are genuinely interested. This is in direct contrast to many conversations where we are simply waiting, patiently or impatiently, to say what we think and are not always that interested in hearing another person's ideas. Most people's default experience is of not being listened to at any level.

Listening involves not just attending to what the person is saying, but noting what they are not saying. Skilled listeners become aware of gaps, pauses, silences, hesitations, and avoid filling this space with their own words. As a consequence, people often say much more as they sense we are attuned to them at a depth that is unusual. Many people have developed these skills without realising how powerful they can be. 'Listening' to the person's body language provides additional information. We can become aware of how a participant communicates not so much by what they say, but by what they convey through their movements and expressions. We often note people's body language without being consciously aware that we are doing this. We notice, without consciously thinking about it, whether they seem relaxed, tense or anxious. As Freud once said:

I set myself the task of bringing to light what human beings keep hidden within … by observing what they say and what they show. I thought the task was a harder one than it really is. He that has eyes to see and ears to hear may convince himself that no mortal can keep a secret. If his lips are silent, he chatters with his fingertips; betrayal oozes out of him at every pore. And thus the task of making conscious the most hidden recesses of the mind is one which it is quite possible to accomplish.

(Freud, 1905: 77–78)

While Freud had the advantage of seeing his patients up to five times a week, skilled listeners are able to pick up these non-verbal cues in any research context. We observe whether people are able to maintain eye contact or need to look away. Being looked at by another person can trigger powerful feelings, leading to a greater ability to trust or, depending on the person, a sense of shame. This is especially important if we are researching a sensitive subject, such as a person's experience of abuse. A research participant's inability to engage in more than just the fleeting eye contact due to a level of internalised shame that is triggered in certain contexts may leave us floundering as we often expect such eye contact to reassure us that everything is fine. In Western culture, being able to hold the gaze of another is a social and interpersonal skill that is required in most important contexts. So much so we need to be reminded that in some non-Western cultures it can be seen as disrespectful to look directly at someone who is an older, wiser person or of a different gender.

Listening at depth is best practice for research and demonstrates a living out of relational ethics. However, research participants can recall being not listened to by their researcher, which left them with feelings of ambiguity about the process. Thinking about psychoanalytic practice, Akhtar (2012) identifies six reasons why an analyst may listen poorly to their patient, and these apply equally to the research context. Akhtar explores 'hearing impairment' (metaphorically) where 'One can hear without listening. But one cannot listen without hearing' (2012: 105). He then adopts the term 'characterological resistance' (2012: 105) to identify that as psychoanalysts span a wider variety of personalities, some may not be predisposed to listen without considerable effort. Some researchers appear to be so focused on the questions they have selected for their research interview that it appears they do not always want to let a conversation develop. Akhtar then turns to 'conceptual rigidity' (2012: 107). Some researchers can find it difficult to let new ideas evolve when their preconceived ideas are challenged, even if they were not fully conscious that they held these ideas in the first place. He moves on to deeper psychoanalytic territory when he offers 'countertransference blocks' (2012: 110). For example, 'the therapist's current financial distress make it hard for him to listen peacefully to his patient's extravagance: it stirred up too much greed' (2012: 112). Other reasons for listening poorly include 'cultural differences' and 'language problems' (2012: 114, 119). All of these can be encountered in the research context and hinder our capacity to listen and engage in the core of relational ethical research.

It is also more difficult if we, as researchers, are interviewing someone who is an expert in their field. This may be experienced through a felt sense of a power imbalance and a concern that we do not have the right to question such a person. Sometimes we can project on to the person we are interviewing a level of status or power that at the same time disempowers ourselves. Clearly, our own personal psychological history and family background, complete with many internalised authority figures who can make themselves felt in unwelcome ways, can have an impact on how we respond to others. So it is important to remember that the person we are involved with in our research may welcome this prospect of thinking for themselves with somebody else and may be grateful for the opportunity to contribute to another person's research. Even apparently more powerful people are still human and have stories to tell.

A therapeutic skills warning

Each professional group, whether nursing, social work or counselling, has established ways of working that over time have become so much a part of us that we do not even have to think about them. Every professional will have a default pattern of engagement with other people, whether they are colleagues, clients or patients. The more developed those therapeutic skills are, the greater the likelihood that a therapeutic engagement with people is unconsciously adopted as a default pattern. This is a reminder that a research relationship involving people-to-people engagement, while enhanced by listening and responding skills, is not a therapeutic relationship.

Our use of such therapeutic skills can lead the people we are researching to disclose more about themselves, their ideas, feelings or experiences than they might otherwise have been comfortable about revealing. Therapists are often skilled at engaging with a person's defence mechanisms, which can become dismantled or circumvented. Everyone uses defence mechanisms to protect a vulnerable sense of self – even if they are experts in their field and have international reputations. There can be moments in a research relationship where, unless we are vigilant about our own processes, we are unconsciously using our therapeutic skills to gain a more detailed insight into the psyche or the personality of the person with whom we are engaged.

A helpful question to ask ourselves as researchers is 'What does it feel like being in this space with my research subject?' Most therapists have had their own personal therapy, worked with a range of clients and have engaged in regular clinical supervision. Through these experiences, they have built up an internal database of thoughts and feelings associated with these respective roles. A researcher is not a pseudo-therapist, patient or supervisor. This is to blur relational boundaries where the ethical frame relates to being a researcher, even if the material is psychologically laden. A relational ethic requires us to respect the other as a research participant. Our responsibility to them is not to be their therapist.

A participatory research relationship

As we saw earlier in this chapter, feminist research has been one of the pioneering strands in the evolution of relational ethics. The purpose of such research is to do something radically different in the acquisition of knowledge. Knowledge is best developed not through an unequal power relationship or an expert/non-expert polarity, but rather through engagement and participation, or, as Benjamin (1988) advocates, 'mutual recognition'. This requires some careful ethical considerations by the researcher about their willingness to use self-disclosure (Oakley, 1981), to allow themselves to become 'the vulnerable researcher' (Etherington, 2009: 70), and to devise ways of co-creating the research with the research participants. Ethical clarity is very important at this point in addressing the issue 'Is this research co-created?' and, if so, 'What are the opportunities and limitations this will impose?' Or is it a philosophical and positioning stance that wants to address power dynamics and imbalances, but does this by greater negotiation, discussion, reflexivity and respect for the other, and still becomes the 'work' owned by the researcher? Benjamin's concept of mutual recognition is helpful here as it locates the differences between the parties involved and does not try to diminish these but forges a bond of mutual respect (see Box 3.6).

BOX 3.6   MUTUAL RECOGNITION

I was interviewed recently by a student completing a thesis for their Master's degree. I had known this student for two years when I had been their tutor on a Diploma course in counselling. Six years had elapsed since then and they were now pursuing another course at a higher academic level. During the interview I was very moved to see that they had been touched by the event I was recalling. As this involved the murder of a close friend, it was a very personal and painful story to tell. Yet I found it very affirming and, despite the former relationship in which there had been a power difference in the student/tutor role, it felt that this was a real meeting that touched both of us – in essence, an I–Thou moment. It was also a moment of mutual recognition.

Transitions in research relationships

At the end of some research projects it becomes evident that a relationship has been made in which there is an ongoing responsibility. Oakley (1981) talks about this in her research with women and their experience of childbirth. Having identified with this research group, she felt she could not simply abandon them. 'Four years after the final interview I am still in touch with more than a third of the women I interviewed. Four have become close friends, several others I visit occasionally, and the rest write or telephone when they have something salient to report, such as the birth of another child' (Oakley, 1981: 46). Oakley and other qualitative researchers argue that 'personal involvement is more than dangerous bias – it is the condition under which people come to know each other and admit others into their lives' (Oakley, 1981: 58). We would go further in saying, following Levinas, that we have a relational and ethical responsibility for others but that there are still issues around ethical boundaries that need recognition. Oakley (1981) gave an example of how her research had relational implications for some of her participants that extended beyond the end of the research process, but note, it was only a third of her former research subjects that maintained contact. Some research requires recognition of the potential for transition, especially if the research area or subject relates to one's professional role or area of expertise. However, this does not mean that a strong bond cannot be created; it simply means that the transition into any future relationship or role requires ethical reflection. An example of such a transition is given in Box 3.7.

BOX 3.7   A RESEARCH RELATIONSHIP TRANSITION

One interviewee subject for my doctoral research was recruited because I had invited them to do a training day for counselling students. During that day we got on very well and so they were able to respond positively to my request for an interview. Again, the interview went well and as we were both involved in the field of psychotherapy and psychoanalysis our paths crossed professionally. When they later developed a new brief form of therapy, I decided to train in this approach, and so a research participant subsequently became my trainer and my clinical supervisor.

Endings in research relationships

Many people find that concluding a relationship, even one that is briefly established or focused around a specific task, can be very difficult, as it often links into our own personal history. Here Freud is very helpful. In a seminal paper 'Mourning and Melancholia' (1917), Freud identified normal grief processes, 'mourning', that can turn to something much more traumatic, 'melancholia'. The catalyst is when we lose part of ourselves that we have invested in other people or particular projects. Research is something that has preoccupied or consumed our time, energy, thinking and feelings, and we can feel lost when it ends. We are left with a mixture of relief and sadness. That same dynamic can be found in research relationships. A real rapport can often be established with a research subject when we engage with them in an interview or focus group setting. This may be less applicable when using research methods without face-to-face contact, yet even here we may have had significant forms of communication with individuals and all concerned can experience feelings of loss when the relationship ends. A helpful and ethical way of concluding a research relationship is to mark both its start and its end by writing to research participants in formal recognition of their contribution. It is a ritual way of acknowledging and ending. Box 3.8 provides an example of a letter sent to participants at the end of a research project.

BOX 3.8   LETTER TO PARTICIPANTS AT THE END OF A RESEARCH PROJECT

Dear Sam,

Thank you for being able to participate in my research project. I enjoyed meeting you in person, so thank you for taking the time to be interviewed. Your contribution has been valuable in identifying new developments in this area, as well as offering new insights. As we agreed at the start of this project, I will send you a summary of the research once it reaches completion. I wish you well as the next stage of life unfolds for you.

Kind regards,
Alistair

This does not preclude further contact or professional relationships evolving, but it is important to let one aspect of a relationship end before any other potential options emerge.

A knowledge of relational ethics and the skills that enable us to form effective relationships enhance the quality of both our ethical practice and our research. However, the more skilled we are at interpersonal relationships, the greater the challenge in terms of avoiding exposing participants to unwarranted intrusion that goes beyond the remit of the research. We also have to be circumspect about developing emotional bonds with participants that endure beyond our projects. While in certain circumstance this is something that can be specifically negotiated as a form of transition, it requires careful reflection and supervision.

The unseen participant

A great deal of the focus on relational ethics has applied to research where there is a face-to-face relationship with participants, but an important relationship still exists, albeit in a different form, in research methods where the researcher and participant do not meet, for example, in questionnaire or online research. This poses considerable challenges in terms of relationship and relational ethics. There still remains the delicate task of creating an emotional bond of sufficient strength that it can bear the burden of the trust required for successful engagement. The person is represented not by their words, as in an interview, but in their data. A questionnaire or virtual or email relationship does exist, and brings with it the same ethical responsibility and a commitment to the same level of care for the participants. This includes ensuring that: they have clear information; they give informed consent; data is securely stored; there is no misinterpretation of data; and they receive feedback. The essential factor is that participants are held in mind as actual people rather than as raw statistical data to be analysed.

REFLECTIVE QUESTIONS

- What skills do you have that would aid your interactions with participants?
- How might these skills complicate the researcher role?
- What factors do you feel are important in building a research relationship?
- Do you feel that research supervision should include a form of emotional support?
- How would you respond if a participant suggested that you meet them socially on another occasion?
- Under what circumstances would you continue to see a participant beyond the end of your research study?

References

Akhtar, S. (2012). *Psychoanalytic Listening: Methods, Limits and Innovations*. London: Karnac.

Allmark, P. (1995). Can there be an ethics of care? *Journal of Medical Ethics*, 2(1): 19–24.

Baier, A. (1985). *Postures of the Mind: Essays on Mind and Morals*. London: Methuen.

Becker, L. and Becker, C. (2003). *A History of Western Ethics*. London: Routledge.

Benjamin, J. (1988). *The Bonds of Love*. New York: Pantheon Books.

Bergum, V. and Dossetor, J. (2005). *Relational Ethics: The Full Meaning of Respect*. Hagerstown, MD: University Publishing Group.

Bordin, E.S. (1979). The generalizability of the psychoanalytic concept of the working alliance. *Psychotherapy: Theory, Research and Practice*, 16: 252–260.

Bordin, E.S. (1980). Of human bonds that bind or free. Presidential address to the 10th annual meeting of the Society for Psychotherapy Research, Pacific Grove, CA, June.

Bordin, E.S. (1983). A working alliance based model of supervision. *Counseling Psychologist*, 11: 35–42.

Bordin, E.S. (1994). Theory and research on the therapeutic working alliance: new directions. In A.O. Horvath and L.S. Greenberg (Eds.), *The Working Alliance: Theory, Research, and Practice*. New York: Wiley.

Buber, M. (1958). *I and Thou*. New York: Scribner.

Castonguay, L.G., Constantino, M.J. and Holtforth, M.G. (2006). The working alliance: where are we and where should we go? *Psychotherapy: Theory, Research, Practice, Training*, 43: 271–279.

Conti-O'Hare, M. (2002). *The Nurse as Wounded Healer: From Trauma to Transcendence*. Sudbury, MA: Jones & Bartlett.

Denzin, N. and Lincoln, Y. (2011). *The Sage Handbook of Qualitative Research* (4th edition). Thousand Oaks, CA: Sage.

Ellis, C. (2007). Telling secrets, revealing lives: relational ethics in research with intimate others. *Qualitative Inquiry*, 13(1): 3–29.

Ellis, C., Adams, M. and Bochner, A. (2011). Autoethnography: an overview. [40 paragraphs]. *Forum Qualitative Sozialforschung / Forum: Qualitative Social Research*, 12(1): Art. 10. Accessed on 8 October 2012 at http://nbn-resolving.de/urn:nbn:de:0114-fqs1101108

Etherington, K. (2004). *Becoming a Reflexive Researcher: Using Our Selves in Research*. London: Jessica Kingsley.

Etherington, K. (2009). Ethical research in reflexive relationships. In L. Gabriel and R. Casemore (Eds.), *Relational Ethics in Practice: Narratives from Counselling and Psychotherapy*. Hove: Routledge.

Evans, M., Bergum, V., Bamforth, S. and MacPhail, S. (2004). Relational ethics and genetic counseling. *Nursing Ethics*, 11(5): 459–471.

Freud, S. (1905). Fragment of an analysis of case of hysteria. *Standard Edition of the Complete Psychological Works of Sigmund Freud* (Vol. 7). London: Hogarth Press.

Freud, S. (1917). Mourning and melancholia. *Standard Edition of the Complete Psychological Works of Sigmund Freud* (Vol. 14). London: Hogarth Press.

Gabriel, L. and Casemore, R. (Eds.) (2009). *Relational Ethics in Practice: Narratives from Counselling and Psychotherapy*. Hove: Routledge.

Gadow, S. (1999). Relational narrative: the postmodern turn in nursing ethics. *Scholarly Inquiry for Nursing Practice*, 13(1): 57–70.

Gilligan, C. (1982). *In a Different Voice: Psychological Theory and Women's Development*. Cambridge, MA: Harvard University Press.

Gilligan, C., Ward, J. and Taylor, J. (1988). *Mapping the Moral Domain: A Contribution of Women's Thinking to Psychological Theory and Education*. Cambridge, MA: Harvard University Press.

Goldberg, C. (1986). *On Becoming a Psychotherapist: The Journey of the Healer*. New York: Gardener Press.

Gordon, P. (1999). *Face to Face: Therapy as Ethics*. London: Constable.

Hand, S. (Ed.) (1989). *The Levinas Reader*. Oxford: Blackwell.

Hayton, A. (2009). Attachment issues associated with the loss of a co-twin before birth. *Attachment: New Directions in Psychotherapy and Relational Psychoanalysis*, 3(2): 144–156.

Held, V. (1993). *Feminist Morality: Transforming Culture, Society and Politics*. Chicago, IL: Chicago University Press.

Held, V. (2006). *The Ethics of Care: Personal, Political, and Global*. New York: Oxford University Press.

Hennessey, R. (2011). *Relationship Skills in Social Work*. London: Sage.

Hess, J. (2003). Gadow's relational narrative: an elaboration. *Nursing Philosophy*, 4(2):137–148.

Hollway, W. (2009). Applying the 'experience-near' principle to research: psychoanalytically informed methods. *Journal of Social Work Practice*, 23(4): 461–474.

Horvath, A.O. and Symonds, B.D. (1991). Relation between working alliance and outcome in psychotherapy: a meta-analysis. *Journal of Counseling Psychology*, 38: 139–149.

Jackson, S.W. (2001). The wounded healer. *Bulletin of the History of Medicine*, 75(1), 1–36.

Josselson, R. (1996). On writing other people's lives: self-analytic reflections of a narrative researcher. In R. Josselson (Ed.), *Ethics and Process in the Narrative Study of Lives* (Vol. 4). Thousand Oaks, CA: Sage.

Loewenthal, D. and Snell, R. (2003). *Postmodernism for Psychotherapists: A Critical Reader*. London: Routledge.

Lyotard, J.F. (1984). *The Postmodern Condition*. St Paul, MN: University of Minnesota Press.

MacDonald, H. (2007). Relational ethics and advocacy in nursing: literature review. *Journal of Advanced Nursing*, 57(2): 119–126.

Macmurray, J. (1961). *Persons in Relation*. London: Faber & Faber.

Martin, D.J., Garske, J.P. and Davis, M.K. (2000). Relation of the therapeutic alliance with outcome and other variables: a meta-analytic review. *Journal of Consulting and Clinical Psychology*, 68: 438–450.

Mies, M. (1983). Towards a methodology for feminist research. In G. Bowles and R. Duelli (Eds.), *Theories of Women's Studies*. London: Routledge and Kegan Paul.

Noddings, N. (1984). *Caring: A Feminine Approach to Ethics and Moral Education*. Berkeley, CA: University of California Press.

Noddings, N. (2002). *Starting at Home: Caring and Social Policy*. Berkeley, CA: University of California Press.

Nouwen, H.J.M. (1979). *The Wounded Healer*. New York: Darton Longman and Todd.

Oakley, A. (1981). Interviewing women: a contradiction in terms. In H. Roberts (Ed.), *Doing Feminist Research*. London: Routledge and Kegan Paul.

Olesen, V. (2005). Early millennial feminist qualitative research: challenges and contours. In N. Denzin and Y. Lincoln (Eds.), *The Sage Handbook of Qualitative Research* (3rd edition). Thousand Oaks, CA: Sage.

Orange, D. (2010). *Thinking for Clinicians: Philosophical Resources for Contemporary Psychoanalysis and the Humanistic Therapies*. London: Routledge.

Priessle, J. (2007). Feminist research ethics. In S. Hesse-Biber (Ed.), *Handbook of Feminist Research: Theory and Praxis*. Thousand Oaks, CA: Sage.

Ruch, G., Turney, D. and Ward, A. (2010). *Relationship-based Social Work*. London: Jessica Kingsley.

Tillett, R. (2003). The patient within: psychopathology in the helping professions. *Advances in Psychiatric Treatment*, 9: 272–279.

Ward, P. (Ed.) (2012). *Perspectives on Ecclesiology and Ethnography*. Grand Rapids, MI: William B. Eerdmans.

Wheeler, S. (2007). What shall we do with the wounded healer? The supervisor's dilemma. *Psychodynamic Practice: Individuals, Groups and Organisations*, 13(3): 245–256.

Zimmermann, J. (2007). Meaning, hermeneutics, and ethics: post-postmodern subjectivity. *International Journal of Existential Psychology and Psychotherapy*, 1(2): 1–9.

4

Establishing trust: the fundamental ingredients

This chapter considers the all-important issue of trust and how it can be established and maintained during the research process. We will explore the ethics of trust and how knowledge of this area can underpin the practical actions that are necessary to establish a trusting relationship. This theoretical aspect is intertwined with the very practical issues of gaining the required permissions and consent, and ensuring that anonymity, confidentiality and data protection are maintained. Permission to proceed is needed not only from participants, but also from any organisations that may be involved directly or indirectly in the research project. We consider the meaning of consent and how reliable consent can be established. We also debate the extent to which confidentiality and anonymity can be maintained within the research process. The chapter discusses issues of data protection and concludes by considering the factors that may undermine trust. This chapter also includes examples of permission processes and checklists to aid putting the matters discussed into practice.

The ethics of trust

What is trust? How can we best describe this somewhat nebulous concept?

> Trust materialises reliably among people to the extent that they have beliefs about one another that make trust a sensible attitude to adopt. And trust reliably survives among people to the extent that those beliefs prove to be correct.
>
> (Pettit, 1995: 202)

Pettit captures the delicate nature of trust in the word 'materialises'. It is as if it is established as a consequence of other things – it cannot be approached directly. In the previous chapter the ethical nature of the relationship between the researcher and the participant was explored. A central factor that underpins the relationship and the whole research endeavour is trust. Research can only proceed if participants trust that they will not be manipulated or viewed as an exploitable means to an end. Gross exploitation in research is rare as it is usually readily identifiable and avoided, but there are subtler forms of exploitation that can undermine trust. Some of these are acts of commission, such as applying pressure to participate or giving participants incomplete information. Some are acts of omission, such as not maintaining adequate contact or failing to provide opportunities for participants to withdraw from the research process. All these types of action can lessen the degree of trust that exists within the research relationship. This chapter considers the nature of trusting relationships, the elements that underpin them and the practical actions within the research process that are necessary to build trust.

The nature of trust

Trust itself cannot be said to be an ethic but results from an ethical relationship. Trust depends on the assessment of a person as to whether another is likely to be trustworthy in their actions. It is not a concept that is easily defined but Reemtsma (2012) captures its complexities effectively:

> What does it mean to be trustworthy? We are trustworthy when we keep our promises, the implicit as well as the explicit. But this is only half the story. We wouldn't call someone trustworthy who threatens to hurt us and then makes good on it. Reliability alone does not make a person trustworthy. Being trustworthy is not only about keeping promises; it means refraining from saying and doing certain things. No less important than knowing what to expect from a person is knowing what not to expect.

(Reemtsma, 2012: 14)

Trust is immensely important and society would be unable to function without it as it facilitates social cohesion (Fukuyama, 1995; Gambetta, 1988). Reemtsma (2012) views it in terms of interpersonal dynamics and maintains that it is established between people through a process of rational decision making. Trust has to be *built* between people and in the initial stages of a project the research participant will be making an active decision about the trustworthiness of the researcher.

Giddens (1990) describes an additional form of trust that exists in relation to institutions. Institutions can build reputations for fair practice. We place our trust in them and assume that all the individuals that are involved with these particular institutions will behave well towards us. If we take Giddens' view, it follows that the research relationship does not begin from a point of zero trust. Researchers, who are members of the caring professions, benefit from three forms of pre-existing trust within society. They are representatives of three types of institution that have already built up trusting relationships with the general public. First, they are regarded as professionals. Professionals are trusted because they are committed to a high standard of conduct that is regulated by professional and statutory bodies. Members of the professions are considered to have a vocation that is underpinned by a higher moral purpose and that stands above economic and individual gains. There is also an assumption that professionals will be reliable. Secondly, they are members of their particular caring profession. The reputation of particular professions, such as nursing, counselling and social work, generates confidence – selflessness and caring are part of their image. Thirdly, they benefit from the reputation of the institution within which they are conducting the research. Institutions involved in research, such as universities, carry with them expectations of fair practice, an adherence to intellectual rigour, and high standards of conduct. Of course the public standing of individual professions and institutions waxes and wanes over time, but there is an enduring overall assumption that associates the professions and academic institutions with ethical practice. There is an implicit assumption that members of these establishments can be trusted.

Individual researchers therefore have trust 'capital' as a starting point, but this exists alongside the assessment that the participant will be making of the particular researcher that they are encountering. For pre-existing trust to be maintained, the individual researcher has to demonstrate that they are a trustworthy person and trust has to be actively worked on to be sustained. As Hodge and Gostin (2008) observe, it only takes one failure for trust to be brought into question. Trust is fragile; it is easily broken.

In thinking about trust, a good starting point is Kant's categorical imperative: 'act only on that maxim that you can at the same time will to be a universal law' (Kant, 1993 [1785]: 30). Although the categorical imperative has been challenged in its applicability to all maxims (Honderich, 1995), an example of a categorical imperative that stands Kant's test is 'Do as you would be done by'. Asking ourselves 'Would we be content if others acted towards us in this way?' is an excellent test for our actions. There is a further aspect of Kant's philosophy that is important in the understanding of trust. He emphasises the pre-existence of freedom for the exercise of individual autonomy to take place. In research terms, this means that it is necessary to ensure that the conditions are in place for participants to be able to make autonomous decisions. This provides us with a further question: 'Are we conducting the research process in ways which facilitate or compromise participants' ability to make independent, informed decisions?'

It is also evident that trust involves an asymmetrical relationship and this has implications for the power dynamic between the participant and the researcher. Trust always involves risk for the truster (Luhmann, 1988). The truster is making a decision to subject themselves to the risk that the other person will abuse their power (Hardin, 1993). The participant, in placing trust in the researcher, is making themselves vulnerable. They are relying on the researcher and the researcher has to be aware of, and take responsibility for, the trust that is placed in them. To assume the existence of an equal power relationship would involve a denial of the nature of the trusting relationship.

Pettit (1995) identifies three beliefs on the part of the person who is trusting. They believe that the person they are trusting is loyal, virtuous and prudent, and these beliefs sustain trust. Participants' pre-existing trust in professionals is based on the beliefs that professionals are loyal to their clients and patients, they have a strong moral basis to their motivation which would make it difficult for them to be untrustworthy, and they exercise caution in their actions. It is also based in an understanding that professionals are bound by codes of ethics.

A further noteworthy aspect of trust is that it is a dynamic entity. Horsburgh (1960) and Pettit (1995) underline its interactive, reinforcing nature and argue that trust 'induces moral goodness' (Horsburgh, 1960: 349). The fact that the researcher is trusted by the participant gives the researcher an impetus to behave in a trustworthy manner and a virtuous circle of trustworthiness is created. The good opinion of others matters to professionals and this is part of their motivation. It could be said that trust is pivotal to the existence of the professions. Committing an untrustworthy act not only reflects negatively on the individual researcher, but also impacts on the reputation of professionals in general, and that of their particular profession and their institutions. It is sobering to note that when a person in a position of trust betrays trust, greater harm results (Freyd et al., 2005), and faith in humanity is diminished.

The capacity that individuals have to exercise trust within relationships has its foundations in their psychological history. People who have healthy attachment patterns are more likely to be able to trust both themselves and others. As a consequence, they may more readily engage with researchers and provide more open responses to research questions because of their inherent capacity to trust. This greater capacity to trust places a responsibility on the researcher not to take advantage of it by ensuring that the participant fully understands the consequences of their participation. Conversely, lack of trust might arise not from the actions of the researcher, but from early or past experiences of trust being broken.

Actions that facilitate trust

How, then, can researchers achieve and sustain trusting relationships with their research participants? Several aspects of the research process have pivotal roles in the creation and maintenance of trust. These are reliability, informed consent, avoiding undue pressure through the use of incentives, a transparent permission process, and the maintenance of confidentiality and anonymity.

Reliability

Here we are referring to basic reliability rather than statistical reliability. The basis of being a reliable researcher lies in being punctual, honouring promises and having good administrative systems in place so that each participant's details are securely kept and the communications with them flow in the correct order and at the right time. This is fundamental in avoiding mistakes and it is essential to spend time thinking about how the administrative aspects of the research process will be managed. Information kept on random scraps of paper in heaps on cluttered desks may not be the most effective way of working. Ensuring that you back up computer-held data and are well prepared for contact with participants is also important, as the researcher in Box 4.1 found to their cost.

BOX 4.1 MISMANAGEMENT

I usually make sure I have copies of everything but this time the only record of my participant's address was in an email that I had stored under a particular email file on my university email system. In a rush to get to the city where I was to interview the participant, I
had forgotten to print out the email. I was due to visit him at home at midday and it was
only during the train journey that I realised my error. I didn't have his address with me
and I had no idea what it was. On arrival, I found an internet café but I could not access
my university's email system. It was unobtainable. I phoned home and my partner managed to find the person's email address via his organisation and emailed him, explaining
the problem and giving my mobile number. The participant was asked to phone me with
the address if he saw the email in time. I sat on a bench outside the station and waited
for three hours. I never heard from him again, despite sending a further apology the next
day. This happened ten years ago but I still feel mortified when I think about it. I had
wasted the participant's time and they must have thought that I was a complete idiot.
Through my carelessness, I lost a valuable participant, a day's work and the train fare.

Reliability also applies to ensuring that enough attention is paid to the technical aspects
of the research process. Unfortunately, equipment failures are not rare happenings.
Completing what initially appear to be straightforward goals and tasks can be demanding in their own right (see Box 4.2).

BOX 4.2 THE BEST LAID PLANS...

Researchers tell anxiety-provoking stories of recording equipment failure, so I used
two different pieces of equipment. In one particular interview both failed because the
record button on one digital recorder was very small and despite pressing it, clearly I
did not do it sufficiently. The other equipment used mini-discs and because a previous
interview had gone on longer than planned, the disc ran out of space.

Informed consent

In order for a participant to make a valid decision to participate they need to know exactly
what kind of commitment they are making and what the research process will involve.
Informed consent is a critical factor in maintaining trust and it has its philosophical basis
in the principle of autonomy. It respects the rights of participants to make independent
decisions. The ability to give informed consent rests on three requirements. The person
must be well-informed, they must have the capacity to make decisions, and they must be
making the decision voluntarily (Brock, 2008). We have discussed the issues of capacity
and voluntariness in Chapter 2 in the section on vulnerable research participants, so we
will focus here on what it means to be well informed. A question that often arises for

researchers is how much information is needed? There are two legal standards for this. First, information should be given at the level that a reasonable person would expect. Secondly, it should be of a professional practice standard, giving the level of detail that most professionals would provide in similar circumstances (Brock, 2008). Transparency and clarity are key. To establish and maintain trust there must be no ambivalence or ambiguity. Additionally, what is being asked of the participant should be reasonable as 'trust only works when not unduly burdened' (Reemtsma, 2012: 45). Therefore the information given to participants must be relevant and easy to understand and they should be encouraged to ask questions. Box 4.3 lists the things that should be made clear.

BOX 4.3   INFORMATION ABOUT THE RESEARCH STUDY

The purpose of the research and why it is being undertaken

What the research process will involve

Any positive aspects or benefits that may occur

Any risks, possible harm or discomfort involved

Clarity about the fact that it is research and not a form of therapy

The extent of confidentiality and anonymity, and the safeguards that will be in place to maintain them

Data storage precautions

The involvement of any third parties (for example, supervisor, translators, transcribers or data consultants)

How and when the data will be destroyed

The level of contact with the researcher

The support that will be available

The right to refuse to answer questions

The right to withdraw participation

The means of distributing the findings to participants

The contact details of the institution, researcher and their supervisor

The complaints procedure

A frequently encountered area of concern for researchers is the recruitment of participants. If participants are slow to materialise, then anxiety levels can be raised and researchers sometimes start to think about offering some form of incentive to ensure an adequate number of participants. However, the use of incentives is a complex area and raises a number of ethical concerns as it is likely to distort the ability of the participant to give unfettered consent.

Avoiding undue pressure through the use of incentives

Incentives are used when there is a concern that recruitment by voluntary methods may not be possible. They are used to encourage participation and can be said to induce motivation to participate. Compensation for lost work time and the reimbursement of travel expenses can be sound and fair practices, but larger monetary or other types of incentive are ethically problematic. Finding the right balance can be difficult. Payment for participation in research with populations from backgrounds of poverty may influence their decision to participate. Their need for money may encourage them to take part in a study that they would not contemplate if their financial circumstance were different. A large reward may also distort the research by subtly encouraging the participant to 'give good value' by embellishing experience or pleasing the researcher by producing and emphasising what they think the researcher wants to hear. It may also undermine the participant's right to withdraw from the study at any point in time as a monetary reward or similar form of incentive may make participants feel that they have received a 'wage' and therefore must complete their 'contract' to participate.

It can be seen that incentives are not simply rewards for time given or a straight-forward economic transaction. They can be part of a power transaction and can induce a 'corruption of judgement' (Grant and Sugarman, 2004: 733). There is an opposing view that says that the corruption of judgement argument denies participants their ability to make autonomous decisions and is paternalistic (Macklin, 1981, 1982), but this form of argument bases the incentive transaction in economic terms and does not give due weight to the underlying power relations that are involved.

> Where participants are hard to recruit and there is thus the greatest need for incentives, one ought to be most reluctant to offer them. The need for large incentives can be a rough indicator that there may be an ethical concern that requires attention. We might say as a rule of thumb that, if you cannot secure participation without offering large incentives, people probably have strong aversions to the study.

(Grant and Sugarman, 2004: 734)

While the arguments against providing financial incentives are strong, there are some settings in which the issue becomes more complex, as without an incentive it may not be possible to carry out the research. For example, when trying to conduct research with people who are homeless and who are addicted to drugs or alcohol, it can be difficult to find participants without offering some form of incentive. This can create a serious dilemma as the researcher may fear that by giving participants money they may be fuelling their addiction. The question here is could the knowledge be gained by any other means? If not, is the risk of facilitating a particular participant's addiction outweighed by the usefulness of the knowledge that will be gained in helping people avoid addiction and homelessness in the future?

It can be seen, then, that incentives are freighted with implications for participants and the research process. Grant and Sugarman (2004) have devised a useful checklist to aid decision making in this area (see Box 4.4).

BOX 4.4   INCENTIVES CHECKLIST

Incentives are problematic when:

Ease of voluntary exit from the study is compromised

There is a dependency relationship with the researcher

There is a high level of risk to the participant

The research may be degrading or shaming

The incentive has to be large to overcome participants' aversion to the study

The aversion is based on participants' principles

The research may cause participants harm

(Grant and Sugarman, 2004: 732)

A transparent permission process

How can we be sure that participants really are consenting to participate in our research? Institutions often insist, quite rightly, on a signed consent form. However, this can result in an over-emphasis being placed on the act of signing for consent. Signing the consent to participate form usually happens when the researcher and the participant meet face to face, and this is usually just prior to the interview or research intervention. It is often the first time that they actually meet. West (2002: 264) warns against 'hit and run' research where the face-to-face meeting is the sole contact that the researcher has with the participants. It is important that the act of signing a consent form is not confused with the process of obtaining consent (Brock, 2008; Wendler and Rackoff, 2001).

It has been argued that informed consent can only be achieved through process permission. This means that the participant is asked if they are willing to participate and to continue to participate at several points along the research process. They are given time to think things through and to realise fully the impact on themselves of each stage of the research process. For example, they may begin to feel uncomfortable about what they have said in an interview several weeks after the event and process permission gives them a further opportunity to modify the data. Process permission was first proposed in nursing research by Munhall (1988), and Grafanaki (1996) has drawn it to the attention of counselling and psychotherapy researchers. Confirming consent on separate occasions ensures more 'protection and freedom of choice for participants' (Grafanaki, 1996: 333). Two examples of permissions processes follow. The first (Box 4.5) illustrates the process for quantitative, experimental research designs that involve a low-risk medical intervention. The second example (Box 4.6) describes the permissions process for a qualitative interview-based study.

BOX 4.5   A RESEARCH PERMISSIONS PROCESS FOR NEUROSCIENCE EXPERIMENTS INVOLVING A VERY LOW MEDICAL RISK

Advertisements with a brief description of the research study are distributed throughout the university requesting volunteers aged 18–25. Reimbursement is offered for volunteers' time and travel expenses. The people who express interest are then given very detailed information about the research and very clear information about the risks that might be involved. They are also told that they will be medically screened to ensure that they are in good mental and physical health before being accepted as a volunteer participant. Potential volunteers are then asked to complete a screening form. If no contra-indications to their participation are detected, they are then invited to attend an induction session.

At the induction session the screening form is completed again as it has been found that the presence of a researcher results in a fuller disclosure of any possible issues that might indicate some form of contra-indication. If nothing significant is found, the participant is medically screened. If they pass all the safety screening processes, they are asked to complete a consent form for the particular experimental technique being used. They also complete another consent form which specifically gives permission for the participant's data to be stored centrally. Because of the need to link to medical records data is not anonymised but kept confidential with the use of secure computing systems. No identifying material is ever published. Participants can request copies of their own data and copies of any publications produced.

Following the experiment participants complete a standard debriefing process, and the details of the particular experiment and the overall purpose of the research is explained again. They are screened post-experiment and asked to return to the unit if they experience any symptoms. If any symptoms are greater than mild, they are not allowed to continue to participate and any adverse effects that warrant exclusion are reported to the university ethics committee.

BOX 4.6   A QUALITATIVE RESEARCH PERMISSIONS PROCESS

The initial recruitment material (flyers and email requests) briefly explained the project. Full details were given to prospective participants prior to their interviews. The aims and scope of the research project were included and questions answered (by email or telephone). It was explained that neither they nor their employers would be identifiable from the research report. Participants were forewarned that the interviews would be digitally recorded in order to give them time to think about the implications of being recorded. At this point a copy of the consent form was emailed to them so that they could read it and consider if they wanted it to be altered in any way. They were encouraged to raise any further questions or concerns they might have. It was also emphasised that they could refuse to answer questions, withdraw from the research, or ask for data to be removed at any time up to one month before the submission of the dissertation.

(Continued)

(Continued)

These safeguards were reiterated at the beginning of the interview and an opportunity given for questions. Each participant was then asked to read/reread and sign the consent form. It was made clear that the recording could be switched off, on request, at any point during the interview. At the end of the interview each participant was asked to confirm that the recording could be used for the research. They were also asked if they would like any sections of the recording deleted. They were offered copies of the recording.

They were told that transcriptions of the interviews would be made and sent to participants so that they could check what they had said. A further opportunity was given to delete any sections that they were concerned about. They were also asked if they still wished to continue to participate in the research. I undertook to destroy the recordings and transcriptions after the examination of the thesis was completed. Participants were given my contact details and were assured that they could contact me at any point if they wished to do so. They also had the contact details of my supervisor. As promised, at the end of the research process and on the completion of my dissertation I sent them a short summary of the research findings and offered to answer any questions that arose from this.

While process permission is effective in maintaining trust and is an important advancement on the one-off permissions event, informed consent has been described as a 'slippery notion' (Renold et al., 2008). What Renold et al. mean by this is that it is difficult at the beginning of a research process to say with complete confidence exactly what participation will involve. This is true both for the research process and for the participant themselves. Research processes may take unexpected directions and this is especially true of exploratory research where the researcher may find that completely unexpected terrain is discovered. Research participants may also find that the research process is having an impact on them that neither they nor the researcher had anticipated. Eisner (1991) points out that the fundamental basis of informed consent is that it is possible to know all the eventualities before the event. Eisner argues that it is not always possible to inform because we simply do not know in detail what will happen. Recognising this problem, Renold et al. (2008) urge researchers to adopt a stance of reflexive praxis and take a more fluid approach to informed consent. This involves paying close attention to the power relations that play out between the researcher and the participant. Consent is regarded as an issue that is in constant negotiation between researcher and participant. In practice, this means maintaining an awareness of the dynamics of the relationship, paying attention to any hesitations or dissonances, and checking for understanding and permission to proceed at regular intervals.

The maintenance of confidentiality and anonymity

The maintenance of effective confidentiality and anonymity underpins trustworthiness. First, it is necessary to distinguish between confidentiality and anonymity. Confidentiality relates to all the information that must remain known only to the researcher. Anonymity relates to disguising or deleting any references to identifying factors to ensure that the participant's identity, or that of any third person, group or institution, is not disclosed when the data is published. It is important not to promise to keep data confidential. The data can be anonymised, but it will be accessible to the public unless special restrictions are placed on access to the research results. The issues that have to remain confidential are those aspects of the data that the participant decides that they do not wish to be included and the things that the participant may have disclosed outside the research data collection method. Only those items that the participant has expressly given consent for can be included in the data for analysis. If an interesting comment is made after the recording has been switched off following an interview, it is necessary to ask separately if it can be included in the data.

Usually, one of the most important things to be kept confidential is the participant's identity. This is done by taking great care that any communications containing their name and personal details and recordings are securely stored in a locked cabinet or password-protected on a computer. Participants are usually assigned a false name or number for the purposes of data processing and discussion with supervisors and consultants. In all usual circumstances, no one other than the researcher needs to know their names. All identifying factors relating to location, institution, names of third parties and any other means by which identity may be guessed are removed or given alternative descriptors from transcriptions or other materials. It is important that if transcribers or other people are to be involved in the processing of the research data, this is made clear to the participant and a contract agreeing to confidentiality is made with the third party concerned.

Confidentiality is a fundamental aspect of a trusting relationship. The participant needs to feel sure that if they wish some aspect of their lives to remain confidential, then this will be respected. A breach of confidentiality may cause real harm to the participant or someone connected to them.

A further aspect related to confidentiality and anonymity is to ensure that the location where the research takes place is free from any risk of the participant being identified by anyone that could later cause them harm. This would be important, for example, in situations of domestic abuse, bullying, or research into organisational factors. Participant safety is paramount and if this is not safeguarded they may be risking physical and mental harm or their future career and reputation.

Having underlined the need for confidentiality and anonymity, it is important to note that, in some forms of research, some participants, for a variety of valid reasons, will actively want their participation to be made known. In these situations the researcher's responsibility lies in endeavouring to ensure that the participants and organisations concerned understand fully any possible negative consequences of waiving anonymity, so that they can balance this against the positive gains. Above all, unless there are strong reasons to the contrary, the participants' final decision should be respected.

Data protection

As well as maintaining sound ethical practice it is also important to be mindful that any data kept on people must also comply with the Data Protection Act 1998. Advice on data storage and regulations can be obtained from the information commissioner's office or via the data protection website (www.dataprotection.gov.uk). People working in the health service and local authority social care settings must also abide by the Caldicott principles (Department of Health, 1997). The Caldicott Committee was set up in 1997 to enquire into the protection of personally identifiable information within the health service. The report was published in 1997 and the recommendations were implemented in 1998. In 2000 the Caldicott Standards (see Box 4.7) were extended to encompass local authorities with social service responsibilities.

BOX 4.7   THE CALDICOTT STANDARDS

1   Justify the purpose(s) of using confidential information.
2   Only use it when absolutely necessary.
3   Use the minimum that is required.
4   Access should be on a strict need to know basis.
5   Everyone must understand his or her responsibilities.
6   Understand and comply with the law.

(Department of Health, 1997)

What undermines trust?

So far we have focused on the elements of research practice that underpin a trusting relationship. Failure to adhere to good practice will impact negatively on trust, but there are additional issues that can undermine trust. These are deception, dual relationships and conflicts of interest.

Deception

Deception in research can result from omission or commission. Omission involves failing to tell the participants important information about the research project. Deception by commission involves deliberately giving participants false information. This can range from telling participants an outright falsehood, such as giving a completely different explanation about the purpose of the research, or misleading them about the research process, to being vague about the area of study when the researcher knows that there will be a specific focus (for example, telling young people that you are researching leisure lifestyles when your focus is really on illegal drug use). Deception undermines trust and it may well harm the individual whose autonomy has been violated. Shipley warns that: '[I]t is seldom possible to overcome the sense of overt betrayal which must ensue … when … one had volunteered for one thing and been used for another' (Shipley, 1977: 102). When deceived, the participant is not in a position to assess the risks involved in the research or give informed consent. Deception also has the capacity to undermine trust in research generally and the researcher's profession.

There is, however, some controversy about whether deception is always unethical (Bok, 1999; Christensen, 1988; Kimmel, 2011). It has been suggested that there may be some instances where deception could be acceptable if it does not cause harm to the participants and there is a strong, ethically-sound argument for not disclosing the research focus. In his paper on social work research ethics, Butler (2002) says that 'only in cases where no other strategy is feasible, where no harm to the research subjects can be foreseen and where the greater good is self-evidently served are procedures involving deception or concealment permissible...' (Butler, 2002: 246). If a form of deception is to be used, then it is essential to ensure that no short-term or long-term damage will be caused to the participants. Ivanoff et al. (2008) underline that deception is likely to be psychologically harmful if it 'causes or encourages participants to react in ways they might not otherwise, or is at odds with important self-attributes (such as kindness to others)' (Ivanoff et al., 2008: 48). Deception in research is a highly controversial area. If you are planning to use it, seek very wide professional consultation and be sure of your ethical ground.

Another form of deception is the falsification of data. While gross dishonesty in terms of data falsification is rare, it has occurred, and occasionally on a grand scale. An academic was identified by the Japanese Society of Anaestheologists as having falsified the data underpinning over 100 papers (Cyranoski, 2012). Fang et al. (2012) have examined the reasons for the retraction of 2,047 published bio-medical and life-science articles and concluded that in 67.4% of cases there was evidence of some form of misconduct. The mistrust that these kinds of actions generate affects not only the reputation of the individual, but also impacts on their organisation and their profession. An even more important factor is the harm that may have resulted from the application of knowledge derived from false data.

Generally, examiners and journal reviewers are used to reading large amounts of research and have a well-honed ability to spot data that does not ring true. In relation to small-scale studies, data falsification is often a panic response to time pressures. Research rarely proceeds smoothly and recruitment difficulties are frequently encountered. Illnesses and personal issues disrupt schedules and computer failures and errors do happen. Planning ahead and leaving space for unexpected delays and interruptions that occur avoids panic situations. An external examiner relates their experience of falsification of data in Box 4.8.

BOX 4.8   THE MISSING INTERVIEWS

In a previous role as an external examiner I was once presented with a challenging issue. A course tutor was suspicious of the qualitative data derived from six interviews that had been used in a Master's dissertation. In reviewing this dissertation I agreed with this suspicion, as I could not see how the quoted data matched up with the analysis. The

(Continued)

(Continued)

student was therefore asked to submit the transcripts of the research interviews. With considerable reluctance the student submitted the data. This consisted of one page of verbatim text and three pages of draft notes taken from one interview. The other five interviews did not exist and it was evident that the material in the dissertation had been fabricated. In a subsequent meeting with the tutor, the student explained that rather than admit that there had been a problem, they had panicked when faced with an impending deadline. As a consequence, they had acted in a grossly unethical manner in fabricating data.

Dual relationships

Dual relationships have long been a thorny issue for counselling and psychotherapy, and so BACP's *Ethical Framework* (2013), for example, is very clear about avoiding this issue with clients. Clearly any type of dual relationship which could be construed as exploitative must be avoided, but there are situations where the issues involved are more complex (Dewane, 2010; Symes, 2003). The question here is should dual relationships always be avoided in research? Are there some forms of dual relationships that might be beneficial?

The tension lies between the absolutist view and the relativist view. The absolutist perspective makes a clear distinction between right and wrong, whereas the relativist view argues that ethical dilemmas should be considered within their particular situations and contexts and the outcome should be judged in terms of the benefit gained (Dewane, 2010). Relativists would argue that pre-existing links do not necessarily involve exploitation. The participants may be known to the researcher professionally, through friendship, or linked through third parties.

Do these types of dual relationship always have a negative impact on the research and its conduct? This is often a concern in areas where the number of people with a particular form of expertise or life experience is very small. For example, if one was to do research on British psychoanalysts, of whom there are fewer than 400, the majority living and working in North London, it would be almost inevitable there would be multiple forms of dual relationships. This seems to be in the very DNA of the psychoanalytic movement itself and it is something that each psychoanalytic association has had to come to terms with. So in each 'scientific meeting', as theoretical discussions are called in the British Psychoanalytic Society, for each trainee psychoanalyst, also present is likely to be their own analyst, their analyst's analyst, their clinical and academic tutors, and the members of the final panel that decide on when they are ready to be called an analyst. This is not problematic as long as a high degree of transparency is maintained and any issues that arise are made explicit and worked through.

When beginning a research project it is important to carry out a pilot project so that the research process and the research materials can be tested. This usually involves two or more participants. An instance of dual relationships sometimes occurs at this point as researchers often feel tempted to use friends and colleagues as the pilot study participants. While the use of colleagues and friends can be helpful in refining the research process, practising interviews, and carrying out research procedures, it is important that a pilot study is also run with 'proper' participants so that the 'real' situation can be reflected on and the process revised as necessary.

Dual relationships are problematic when the pre-existing relationship causes the participant to modify their research responses. If there is a pre-existing hierarchical, professional or social relationship, these factors may impinge on the degree of openness that the participant will engage in. A researcher wondered whether some form of impression management happened when she interviewed a person from her local community about his experience of divorce (see Box 4.9).

BOX 4.9   THE RETICENT PARTICIPANT

I was undertaking a qualitative study about the feelings associated with divorce and the ways in which people had dealt with them. I interviewed 20 people from a wide geographical area. All the participants were unknown to me except for one man who lived locally and had expressed interest in being interviewed when he heard, on the local grapevine, that I was doing this research. When I came to analysing the data it was clear that his interview had produced notably different results from the rest. He had presented himself as being able to manage his emotions very effectively and to avoid any strong feelings of anger, rage, revengefulness, shame or indeed anything very negative. I wondered if being known to me and part of my community made him reticent about being really open. Of course it may be that he did not experience any strongly negative feelings, but my hunch is that he wanted to present a positive view of himself as a highly reasonable person because he would see me in the future at social occasions in the town. I decided that in future research projects I would recruit people unknown to me unless there were very good reasons to do otherwise.

If a participant in a dual relationship does set aside any reticence and is very open with the researcher, then afterwards they may regret it and experience feelings such as shame or have anxieties about how their revelations will influence their future relationship with the researcher.

In contrast to these negative aspects, at times a pre-existing relationship can facilitate very good research. Having established a positive ethical relationship with the participant in one role, for example, as their counsellor, nurse or social worker, this can facilitate a valuable research relationship that is trusting, has a sound ethical basis and is beneficial to both parties. In Chapter 5 we consider the particular form of dual relationship which occurs in case study research, where the research participants are also clients or patients of the researcher concerned.

Conflicts of interest

Emanuel and Thompson (2008) emphasise that integrity and quality should be the primary focus of research and if these issues are brought into question, trust is undermined. A conflict of interest arises when a secondary interest, such as personal advancement or some form of financial reward, unduly influences the conduct of the research. Personal advancement can arise in a variety of forms, such as obtaining qualifications, increasing employability, gaining promotion or enhancing reputation. Financial reward could involve some direct personal gain but may also be linked to obtaining research grants or increasing research budgets. In times of financial constraint, the future of whole departments may depend on sustaining some kind of financial backing. In these circumstances professional judgement may become distorted and secondary interests given undue priority.

Emanuel and Thompson (2008) make the valuable observation that it is important to think of conflicts of interest in terms of tendencies rather than occurrences. We may have little conscious awareness of an insidious form of unethical behaviour that creeps into the decision-making processes. When involved in making research decisions we need to be alert to feelings of dissonance. If they occur, this is the moment to ask: 'What is the primary motivation behind the decision being made?' The answer to this question can be revealing and can help us to stay on the track of quality and integrity. It is also important to note that participants will not be aware of the secondary interests and are unable to assess researchers' underlying motives (Emanuel and Thompson, 2008).

A larger question for researchers from the counselling, nursing and social work professions is: 'Is there a fundamental conflict of interest between being a member of the caring professions and a researcher?' What is the primary obligation here? Is it to the advancement of knowledge or to your fellow human beings? Is there a risk that 'moral sensitivity [could be] clouded by a blind focus on obtaining research results' (Lemmens, 2008: 747)? It can be argued that as a member of one of these professions, we can never let go of our professional obligations and responsibilities. We cannot regard ourselves as 'just researchers'; we have to incorporate all our skills and obligations if we are to maintain trust and integrity.

REFLECTIVE QUESTIONS

- What does it feel like to be trusted?
- What does it feel like to trust someone?
- How does a degree of trust bring about an increased level of ethical responsibility?
- What information do your participants need to have to ensure informed consent?
- Are any dual relationships likely to be involved in your research?
- Would you consider asking a colleague to participate in your research?

References

Bok, S. (1999). *Lying: Moral Choice in Public and Private Life* (2nd edition). New York: Vintage.

British Association for Counselling and Psychotherapy (2013). *Ethical Framework for Good Practice in Counselling and Psychotherapy*. Leicester: BACP.

Brock, D.W. (2008). Philosophical justifications of informed consent in research. In E.J. Emanuel, C. Grady, R.A. Crouch, R.K. Lie, F.G. Miller and D. Wendler (Eds.), *The Oxford Textbook of Clinical Research Ethics*. Oxford: Oxford University Press.

Butler, I. (2002). A code of ethics for social work and social care research. *British Journal of Social Work*, 32: 239–248.

Christensen, L. (1988). Deception in psychological research: when is it justified? *Personality and Social Psychology Bulletin*, 14: 664–675.

Cyranoski, D. (2012). Retraction record rocks community. *Nature*, 489: 7146. Accessed on 1 December 2012 at www.nature.com/news/retraction-record-rocks-community-1.11434

Data Protection Act 1998. London: HMSO. Accessed on 5 December 2012 at: www.legislation.gov.uk/ukpga/1998/29/data.pdf

Department of Health (1997). *Report on the Review of Patient-identifiable Information* (The Caldicott Report). London: Department of Health. Accessed on 5 December 2012 at: www.dh.gov.uk/prod_consum_dh/groups/dh_digitalassets/@dh/@en/documents/digitalasset/dh_4068404.pdf

Dewane, C.J. (2010). Respecting boundaries: the dos and don'ts of dual relationships. *Social Work Today*, 10(1): 18.

Eisner, E. (1991). *The Enlightened Eye: Qualitative Enquiry and the Enhancement of Educational Practice*. New York: Macmillan.

Emanuel, J.E. and Thompson, D.F. (2008). The concept of conflicts of interest. In E.J. Emanuel, C. Grady, R.A. Crouch, R.K. Lie, F.G. Miller and D. Wendler (Eds), *The Oxford Textbook of Clinical Research Ethics*. Oxford: Oxford University Press.

Fang, F.C., Steen, R.G. and Casadevall, A. (2012). Misconduct accounts for the majority of retracted scientific publications. *Proceedings of the National Academy of Sciences of the United States of America*, 109(42): 17028–17033.

Freyd, J.J., Klest, B. and Allard, C.B. (2005). Betrayal trauma: relationship to physical health, psychological distress and a written disclosure intervention. *Journal of Trauma and Dissociation*, 6: 83–104.

Fukuyama, F. (1995). *Trust: The Social Virtues and the Creation of Prosperity*. New York: Basic Books.

Gambetta, D. (1988). Can we trust? In D. Gambetta (Ed.), *Trust: Making and Breaking Cooperative Relations*. Oxford: Blackwell.

Giddens, A. (1990). *The Consequences of Modernity*. Oxford: Polity Press.

Grafanaki, S. (1996). How research can change the researcher: the need for sensitivity, flexibility and ethical boundaries in conducting qualitative research in counselling/psychotherapy. *British Journal of Guidance and Counselling*, 24(3): 329–338.

Grant, R.W. and Sugarman, J. (2004). Ethics in human subjects' research: do incentives matter? *Journal of Medicine and Philosophy*, 29(6): 717–738.

Hardin, R. (1993). The street-level epistemology of trust. *Politics and Society*, 21: 505–529.

Hodge, J.G. and Gostin, L.O. (2008). Confidentiality. In E.J. Emanuel, C. Grady, R.A. Crouch, R.K. Lie, F.G. Miller and D. Wendler (Eds.), *The Oxford Textbook of Clinical Research Ethics*. Oxford: Oxford University Press.

Honderich, T. (1995). *The Oxford Companion to Philosophy*. Oxford: Oxford University Press.

Horsburgh, H.J.N. (1960). The ethics of trust. *The Philosophical Quarterly*, 10(41): 343–354.

Ivanoff, A., Blythe, B. and Walters, B. (2008). The ethical conduct of research. In R.M. Grinnell and Y.A. Urau (Eds.), *Social Work Research and Evaluation: Foundations of an Evidence-based Practice*. New York: Oxford University Press.

Kant, I. (1993 [1785]). *Grounding for the Metaphysics of Morals* (3rd edition). Indianapolis, IN: Hackett Publishing Company.

Kimmel, A.J. (2011). Deception in psychological research – a necessary evil? *The Psychologist*, 24(8): 580–585.

Lemmens, T. (2008). Conflict of interest in medical research. In E.J. Emanuel, C. Grady, R.A. Crouch, R.K. Lie, F.G. Miller and D. Wendler (Eds.), *The Oxford Textbook of Clinical Research Ethics*. Oxford: Oxford University Press.

Luhmann, N. (1988). Familiarity, confidence, trust: problems and alternatives. In D. Gambetta (Ed.), *Trust: Making and Breaking Cooperative Relations*. Oxford: Blackwell.

Macklin, R. (1981). 'Due' and 'undue' inducements: on paying money to research subjects. *IRB: Ethics & Human Research*, 3(5): 1–6.

Macklin, R. (1982). Response: beyond paternalism. *IRB: Ethics & Human Research*, 4(3): 6–7.

Munhall, P.L. (1988). Ethical considerations in qualitative research. *Western Journal of Nursing Research*, 10(2): 150–162.

Pettit, P. (1995). The cunning of trust. *Philosophy and Public Affairs*, 24(3): 202–225.

Reemtsma, J.P. (2012). *Trust and Violence*. Princeton, NJ: Princeton University Press.

Renold, E., Holland, S., Ross, N.J. and Hillman, A. (2008). Becoming a participant: problematizing 'informed consent' in participatory research with young people in care. *Qualitative Social Work*, 7(4): 427–447.

Shipley, T. (1977). Misinformed consent: an enigma in modern society social science research. *Ethics in Science and Medicine*, 4: 93–106.

Symes, G. (2003). *Dual Relationships in Counselling & Psychotherapy: Exploring the Limits*. London: Sage.

Wendler, D. and Rackoff, J. (2001). Informed consent and respecting autonomy: what's a signature got to do with it? *IRB: Ethics & Human Research*, 23(3): 1–4.

West, W. (2002). Some ethical dilemmas in counselling and counselling research. *British Journal of Guidance and Counselling*, 30(3): 261–268.

5

Research dilemmas, decisions and details

Codes of research ethics are useful for guidance and it is important to consult them when beginning a research project. They alert us to things that we may not have previously considered, set standards for good practice and help us to avoid ethical errors. The errors that new researchers make are more usually due to acts of omission rather than commission. They may not have thought through all the various ethical aspects of their research process or they may feel tentative about asking permissions. Effective preparation can enable these kinds of unethical behaviours to be avoided. However, while we can strive to ensure that unethical behaviours and actions do not arise, no matter how good the preparations are, ethical dilemmas will occur during the research process (Lakin, 1988). This is especially true of qualitative research as this type of research is exploratory and it is rarely possible to foresee all the situations and complexities that may arise.

Due to the relational nature of the participant–researcher encounter, as highlighted in Chapter 3, it is evident that moment-by-moment ethical negotiations and decisions are a characteristic of the research relationship. The first part of this chapter returns to principle ethics and explores how ethical principles can be useful in helping the researcher to unravel and resolve ethical dilemmas. The second part of the chapter highlights points in the research process where ethical considerations are likely to be in the foreground.

Ethical dilemmas and the usefulness of principle ethics

How do we know that a research decision is also an ethical decision? Dubois (2008: 46) says that 'decisions fall into the realm of ethics when they pertain to things within our control that will either show respect or fail to show respect to human beings'. He emphasises that a large number of our everyday decisions are actually ethical decisions, but because they are not problematic they are not noticed. However, sometimes it is not clear what the 'right' decision should be and we are faced with a dilemma. In these situations there are 'good, but contradictory ethical reasons to take conflicting and incompatible courses of action' (Kitchener, 1984: 43). Ethical dilemmas may be encountered at any stage of the research process and although professional ethical codes can act as guides, often they do not provide solutions for dilemmas. The decisions involved have to be taken by individual researchers and their advisers. Researchers therefore need to be competent in identifying and weighing up the issues involved in a particular dilemma in order to arrive at the best possible outcome.

Dubois (2008) identifies three varieties of ethical problem. There are problems that are volitional, cognitive or social. A problem is volitional when the researcher knows what the right course of action is. The ethical issue here is whether they will actually do what they know is right. So, for example, I may know that it is likely to be ethically problematic to ask a good friend to be a participant in my research, but because of recruitment pressures will I overcome the temptation to make use of this 'easy' option? I am aware that this action might distort both the quality of the research data and our relationship, but will I make the decision not to interview them? Do I have the moral and emotional strength to refrain from an unethical action?

A cognitive problem exists when the researcher is unsure about the right course of action. For example, is it ethically acceptable to give a participant a gift for their involvement in the research project? Will this be suitable recompense for the time they have given us or will it affect their ability to ask to withdraw their data from the research if they later become uncomfortable at the thought of it being part of published work?

A social problem arises when people or bodies involved in the research study have conflicting needs or expectations. The researcher knows what the right course of action is, but there are social pressures that make them hesitate to act. For example, the research findings may have highlighted poor group therapy outcomes in a voluntary organisation but dissemination of the research may affect donations to that charity, which otherwise does a great deal of good in the world.

The volitional type of ethical problem relates directly to ourselves and depends on the researcher developing their own internal moral compass. We may benefit from the opinions and advice of others, but these ethical decisions largely depend on our own self-awareness and ability to resist the temptation to take unethical short-cuts when under pressure.

For the second two types of dilemmas – cognitive and social dilemmas – it can be helpful to have a framework or method that structures the process of thinking through the issue. Ethical principles can be of use here and help us to consider all the aspects of a particular dilemma in a systematic way.

As described in more detail in the first part of Chapter 1, Beauchamp and Childress (2001) identify four ethical principles. These are beneficence (do good), non-maleficence (do no harm), justice, and autonomy. And there are two later additions: fidelity (faithfulness, engendering trust through ethical behaviour) and veracity (striving to be truthful) (Kitchener, 1984; Meara et al., 1996). An ethical dilemma can be considered in the light of each of these ethical principles to clarify the issues involved. In Box 5.1 a midwife researcher shows how she used the ethical principles to think through the dilemmas related to her research.

BOX 5.1   USING ETHICAL PRINCIPLES TO THINK THROUGH DILEMMAS

As a midwife researcher I was keen to explore the needs of parents who have experienced stillbirth and its impact on their relationships in the first six months following their bereavement. I wanted to use a qualitative interview-based methodology to obtain an in-depth description of their experiences. Before starting the project, I discussed my research proposal with colleagues in my department and with two former patients who had experienced stillbirth and were now fundraisers for equipment for our department. A few of my colleagues, while feeling that the research might help them to improve their practice, raised reservations about the in-depth interviews and were concerned that the parents would be revisiting painful memories that may re-traumatise them. They also questioned whether the research would revive marital difficulties. My discussion with the parents revealed that they felt that better support was needed and that they would be only too pleased to tell their stories if it meant that future parents would get better support.

I felt torn between the two perspectives. I wanted to improve nursing support to future bereaved parents, but also felt anxious about upsetting participants and I was worried that I might make their situations worse because of my research.

As a first step I noted my own response and feelings about the issue. At this intuitive level I felt that it would do more good than harm to undertake the research. I felt that there was a strong need for more detailed information and guidance for nurses, and I was also influenced by the keenness of the parents for the research to go ahead.

Thinking the issues through using the ethical principles in the following way helped to clarify matters.

Beneficence: what good may come out of this research?

- Improved nursing practice – the evidence for the need for this comes from my own clinical experience, and that of the colleagues and, the most important factor, from the parents.
- The parents are keen to tell their stories and would like some good to come out of their painful and distressing experience. They said that if better support for future parents would result from the research then that would be a good reason for them to take part.
- The telling of their stories may in itself be helpful for them – to have the difficulties and pain that they experienced acknowledged.

Non-maleficence: how might my research cause harm?

- The in-depth interviews and reflections on the impact on their relationships may cause re-traumatisation and resurrect relationship difficulties between partners.

(Continued)

(Continued)

Justice

- The parents wanted their voices to be heard and this would give them a sense of recognition and equitable treatment.

Autonomy

- As the parents are keen to tell their stories, their ability to make autonomous decisions should be respected.

Fidelity

- The parents' stories would be faithfully represented. I would take steps to ensure their anonymity and keep any research material secure.

Veracity

- I would be transparent in my dealings with the parents and give them accurate information about the study and any uses that may be made of the data. It was also apparent that the truth of the parents' experience had not been fully acknowledged and the research could help to address this issue.

Having clarified the issues involved, it became clear to me that there were strong reasons for going ahead with the research, but also that if I was to do this I must think my research process through carefully and minimise any possible harm that could arise. I therefore ensured that I developed clear information leaflets about the project; I was forewarned to be alert to any signs of distress in the interviews; and I would also provide my contact details for further questions and discussion. I also included details of local support systems and organisations for bereaved parents and for people who were experiencing relationship difficulties. Before proceeding, I explained my proposed research process to the parents I had consulted and my colleagues, and talked through the extra safeguards that I had put in place. They were pleased with these alterations and confirmed that I should go ahead. Interestingly, going through this process and returning to consult colleagues highlighted two additional issues that I had not considered. First, a colleague wondered whether the participants would like to be referred to as parents or would prefer another term to be used. Secondly, I was asked if I would be aiming to interview both partners of couples, or just interview any individuals who volunteered. These two issues required further thought and discussion.

For those who like to have a more structured framework for working through ethical dilemmas, the 'clarify, consult, consider, choose and check' model (Bond, 1993; Shillito-Clarke, 1996) provides a useful approach. It has been found to be an effective framework for thinking through ethical dilemmas in counselling and psychotherapy practice but can be usefully applied to research dilemmas in other domains (see Box 5.2).

BOX 5.2   THE CLARIFY, CONSULT, CONSIDER, CHOOSE AND CHECK MODEL

Clarify

- Describe the issue as clearly as possible.
- Identify the elements involved.
- Imagine the perspective of each person who may be involved.
- Produce a list of evidence for and against a particular action (at this point you could run through the ethical principle analysis described above).

Consult

- Read the code of research ethics of your relevant professional body and consult any others that you find helpful. These might include the managers of any organisations involved or participant representatives.
- Could there be any legal implications of your actions? If so, consult your organisation, professional body, insurer or a legally qualified person, as appropriate.

Consider

- Discuss the issue with your research supervisor and any suitably qualified and experienced peers. Ensure that you are maintaining appropriate confidentiality.
- Keep notes of these consultations.

Choose

- Select the best action and provide further space for review before action.

Check

- Reflect on the outcome and whether this was the best option.
- What is there to be learned about this situation and yourself?

A similar type of framework is suggested by Dubois (2008). Dubois' form of analysis is called 'So Far No Objections' (this is an acronym to aid in remembering the letters SFNO). His framework is based on a common denominator approach and resembles similar frameworks devised by Thomasma et al. (1995) and Jennings et al. (2003). It uses a root cause analysis and proposes that there are three sources to dilemmas:

1 Different people are involved who have competing interests.
2 Uncertainty or disagreement exists about relevant facts.
3 Uncertainty, conflict or disagreement exists regarding ethical norms.
   (Dubois, 2008: 49)

Dubois suggests collecting and recording the following information:

4   S – Stakeholders: Who will be significantly affected by the decision made? First, consider whether reasons exist for giving priority to the interests of one party over another. Secondly, identify who is invested with decision-making authority.
5   F – Facts: What issues might generate disagreement?
6   N – Norms: What ethical principles, norms or values are at stake? Which are relevant and which generate disagreement?
7   O – Options: What actions or policies deserve serious consideration? If the ethical ideal is not possible, what compromises can be made?
(Summarised from Dubois, 2008: 49)

These useful forms of analysis provide a guide to help researchers make difficult decisions. Having a structure to work through lowers anxiety and ensures a more rigorous decision-making process. Often there is no ideal outcome and it is necessary to choose between strong but different ethical demands. The best we can do is to have thought through an action thoroughly and to have sound reasons to underpin the actions that we have decided to take. Ethical dilemmas can be encountered at any point in the research process and we are now going to look at the different kinds of ethical decisions that need to be made when planning a research study.

Deciding on a research topic

When making the initial decision to research a particular topic, researchers may be so enthusiastically focused on their research idea that they can underestimate the ethical implications of the project. The keenness to investigate a fascinating area, acquire new knowledge, obtain a qualification or write a paper for a journal can blind us to the ethical implications of our investigation. As soon as the idea is formed, the first question should be 'What are the ethical concerns relating to this research investigation?' Two issues are important at this stage. These are preparation and flexibility.

Having identified an area of interest, the next stage is to search the existing literature and discuss the idea with people who are familiar with the topic area. If a gap in knowledge is confirmed, then this is good news but researchers should also entertain the idea that the gap might be there for a reason. They should not be put off their discovery but it is possible that other people have had this idea and have decided that the ethical risks or complexities involved are too great to proceed. Our ideas are often very precious to us and we can become firmly attached to them, but research requires flexibility. It is not unusual for first research ideas to be modified or even substantially changed. The best ethical approach to a topic may not be the way that it was originally envisaged and perhaps modifications will have to be made or even changes to the initial subject area. This can be a painful experience and evoke feelings of anger and resentment towards research supervisors and advisers who suggest a different course of action. Take time to reflect on their advice. The likelihood is that it is sound advice and compromise may provide the best ethical outcome. The student in Box 5.3 chose to go ahead with their plan despite advice to the contrary.

BOX 5.3   THE SUPERVISOR'S PERSPECTIVE

A Master's student wanted to interview adolescents (aged 14–17) whose parents were in prison during their childhood to learn more about the impact that it had on their lives. This idea came from the student's own experience of their father's criminal history and they felt passionate about researching this topic. Although such research could provide valuable data, it was also an ethical minefield that might affect the children themselves, their relationships with their parents, and the parents. There were also concerns about the researcher's personal safety. A further issue was that the researcher had no training in direct work with young people.

The supervisor suggested that a first step in embarking on this kind of research would be to recruit adults for the study who could reflect on the impact of having had parents in prison during their childhood. If the student completed a good Master's study on the data from adults, this could form the springboard for doctoral research, during which they could acquire the necessary training and carefully research a form of methodology to gain the contemporaneous experience of the adolescents which they were originally hoping to capture. The researcher remained wedded to their first idea and, despite the supervisor's advice that the proposal would not pass even the first ethical review stage, the student submitted the proposal. It failed to get ethical approval. The student had to revise the project and resubmit which wasted two months of their valuable research time.

We want to emphasise that we do not think that ethically difficult research areas should be avoided. Starting from a point of thinking through all the possible ethical concerns relating to the project can save time, energy and disappointment. It may be that an ethically complex subject area can be investigated if a particular design or approach to the research is taken. This raises the question whether there are particular ethical concerns associated with different research methods?

Choosing a research method

Each method of investigation has its own particular methodology, that is, its own philosophical and theoretical basis. We may feel personally drawn to a particular method because it fits with our view of the world. For example, we may take a positivist view of the world and favour quantitative research. The position would be taken that knowledge is neutral and separate from the method that is used to produce it, and that researchers can be completely objective in their relation to the research process. This works well for research into physical phenomena. However, when human participants are involved, phenomena may be more difficult to measure in this way due to the complex and multiple nature of the variables. A qualitative approach that acknowledges the subjectivity of the researcher and the socially constructed nature of experience may be more appropriate. If a researcher is so wedded to a particular worldview and imposes it on a subject area that is not well suited to that form of method and underlying philosophy, then the quality of the research will suffer and any practical application of the research findings may cause harm. Retaining an openness to all methods has ethical implications in that selecting the most appropriate method for the topic under investigation means that the best possible data is obtained from participants in the best possible way. The loss of their valuable time and any risks of discomfort through participating are balanced by the best possible outcome being obtained. At times this may involve using a mixed methodology (see Box 5.4).

BOX 5.4   MIXED METHODS

A quantitative statistical analysis of patient recovery and discharge times may show that a particular treatment produces the quickest recovery and discharge time. But interviews with patients who have undergone this treatment reveal that the subjective experience of the technique is distressing and that if they were given the choice they would opt for a slower recovery but a more acceptable procedure. Using both methods gives the fullest picture.

Cooper and McLeod (2010) have advocated a pluralistic approach in relation to counselling and psychotherapy orientations, and their arguments apply equally soundly to research. There are fashions in research, and in recent decades in qualitative research we have seen grounded theory emerge as a dominant methodology, only to be superseded by interpretive phenomenological analysis and thematic analysis. It is also evident that professions can privilege certain forms of enquiry and there are implicit pressures exerted on researchers to conform. At times the pressure can be less subtle. Researchers, aware that a future career in academia depends on publication in peer-reviewed journals, may be influenced by the fact that their professional journals will prioritise, for example, quantitative over qualitative methods.

Sometimes individual researchers become aligned with, and committed to, a particular methodology and will describe themselves, for example, as a quantitative, grounded theory, narrative or phenomenological researcher. While it is good that they have a specialism, it is also important that they focus on research areas that are best served by this method and that they are not engaging in what Salmon (2003) has described as methodologism. By this, he means a devotion to the method where the adherence to it and the particular way of applying the method take precedence over every other aspect of the research process. This may result in paying less attention to participant care and failing to achieve the best possible overall results. When the subject area is decided upon, the goal should be to select the most appropriate and ethically sound way of investigating the chosen topic. We can have preferred research methods but we should aim to remain open to different ways of investigating topics. Methodologies are derived from philosophical ideas and theories; they are not matters of fundamentalist belief. They should be examined as the research proceeds and critiqued for their effectiveness. Methods are the tools of the researcher and they may need sharpening, mending or replacing.

Whatever methodology is utilised, the researcher needs to have had adequate training and be competent in using it. As Rosenthal (1994: 128), a psychologist, remarks, 'bad science makes for bad ethics'. This applies equally to counselling, nursing and social work research. If we do not apply our methodology effectively, we are wasting our participants' time and the results and conclusions of the research are likely to be inaccurate.

Quantitative research

Quantitative research is used extensively in medical, social and psychological settings. It is invaluable in gaining an understanding of behaviours and experiences across large groups of people. The gold standard of quantitative research is the randomised controlled trial. Classically, a randomised controlled trial involves a treatment group and a group that does not receive treatment, know as a 'control group'. There are more complex variations on this pattern so, for example, if it was necessary to carry out research to see which form of therapy was the most effective for people with depression, there might be a group that receives a standard CBT (cognitive behavioural therapy) intervention, a group that has person-centred counselling, a group that has no treatment of any form, and a group that receives medication from their general practitioner. The participants would be measured for their level of depression before and after the treatment/no treatment using a standard depression questionnaire. A statistical analysis of the results would provide an indication of the relative effectiveness of each intervention.

Boruch (1997) argues that randomised trials are ethical because in a state of uncertainty they are the best way of determining how to intervene effectively. Secondly, because of the rigour of the statistical analyses used to test the results, they provide answers with an adequate level of certainty and are a sound basis for positively influencing practice. However, there are a variety of ethical concerns relating to such methods. A concern that has been frequently raised is 'Is it ethical to leave a group untreated when you might be aware that the forms of treatment being tested are effective?' This criticism has been addressed by ensuring that the most effective treatment that the research discovers is given to all the other groups at the end of the trials. Designs that compare two forms of treatment or intervention that are both felt to be effective and do not use a no-treatment group also avoid the dilemma of causing harm by not treating one of the groups.

Boruch (2005) suggests five criteria to justify randomised controlled trials. First, he says that the research needs to address an important problem. Secondly, there is uncertainty about the best course of action. Thirdly, other research methods would not be equally informative. Fourthly, the results will be used to inform practice. Fifthly, participants will be respected and will not be left worse off. In discussing Boruch's first criterion of importance, Mark and Gamble (2009) raise an issue that provides us with food for thought. Who decides that a particular area is important?

Is it policy makers, managers, practitioners or service users? Is it defined as important for economic or practice reasons or for some other form of reason? These are all questions that are worth consideration.

Randomised controlled trials are only one form of quantitative research but they are regarded as the most reliable method and are considered to be the best form of evidence by the National Institute for Clinical Excellence (NICE). It is important that qualitative researchers do not ward themselves off from quantitative research. It is valuable to know with a level of statistical certainty, for example, that CBT is an effective treatment for obsessive-compulsive disorders. However, practitioners may be more interested in the minutiae of the therapeutic effects and change processes, and want to understand in detail how particular forms of intervention are effective. A working knowledge of quantitative methods enables researchers to provide a more effective critique when arguing the case for qualitative methods.

In quantitative research the data can be anonymised by removing names and identifying material. The large data sets involved usually reduce the ethical risks relating to the identification of individuals. A more pertinent ethical question for quantitative researchers is one of fidelity. Am I being faithful to my participants? Having gathered this data from a large number of participants, am I using the most appropriate statistical means of analysis, and am I analysing this data thoroughly enough to do justice to the time and effort that participants gave to the study? Am I getting the greatest amount of good in terms of knowledge and understanding out of this data? Am I conducting the analysis in an open and honest way? If we consider non-maleficence, am I ensuring that there is no form of deception in my manipulation of the data? This also pertains to the presentation of the data. Is the data being presented in a truly representative way? Or is the presentation of data selective and likely to cause people to draw incorrect inferences from the way I am presenting it? Am I presenting my data within the context of my other research projects/experiments in this area or am I highlighting the one 'successful' research outcome and marginalising or failing to report all the other unsuccessful outcomes I have had in the same research area?

Qualitative research

In qualitative work there are similar issues but the emphasis is different. An important ethical issue in qualitative research relates to intrusion. An individual participant may decide that the level of intrusion into a potentially sensitive subject is bearable because of the potential usefulness of the research. In thinking about intrusion, it is useful to consider the difference between disclosure (the controlled and willing relating of personal information) and exposure where the participant is caught off-guard and bounced into saying too much, or their identifying details are not safeguarded well enough and they risk being identified. Participants are usually comfortable with making disclosures but few people are comfortable with exposure. However, they may not fully understand, for example, that their story will be written up in a dissertation that is then available to the public through the library system. While stories can be anonymised, there may still remain the fear that a parent, partner or child, knowing that they have participated in a research project, may read the dissertation and attempt to identify them. When designing a project, key questions are 'Does the participant fully understand what is involved?' and 'What are the risks of intrusion and exposure that the participants may be subject to?' If a sensitive topic is to be explored, it is worth contacting likely participants and any specialists or organisations that have particular knowledge of the research area to ask them if they think that research in the chosen area would be valuable, and, if so, what might be the risks to participants, and what safeguards should be in place to protect or care for participants in the best possible way.

One form of qualitative research raises particular ethical issues. Case study research has been described as the form of research that involves a greater degree of moral risk (McLeod, 2010). Practitioners value case studies as they provide an in-depth examination of the minutiae of practice. They are an essential means of exploring practice and learning from it. Flyvbjerg (2006) argues that this form of research is as valid as any other methodology and provides a valuable contribution to knowledge. However, case studies raise particular concerns as this type of research almost always arises out of a pre-existing professional relationship. The researcher is the practitioner; the participant is the patient/client. There is a unique blurring of boundaries. Several ethical issues present especially complex dilemmas. These are: anonymity, consent, and the impact of the case study on the client/patient, the practitioner and their professional relationship.

In the past, clients and patients were often simply not consulted about the use of their case material. It was assumed that changing names and a few details were adequate safeguards. Even though names and obvious identifying details can be anonymised, there remains the possibility that the detailed history and engagement with the practitioner have a unique pattern that could enable identification by the client/patient or a third party. It is more usual these days for consent to be obtained and we would regard this as essential practice for any form of research case study or publication. However, when the participant has also been the client or patient, is it possible, given the complex dynamics of professional relationships, to give unfettered consent? It has been suggested that final consent should be obtained only at the end of the professional relationship and that it is best managed by someone other than the practitioner (McLeod, 2010). It is also apparent that reading case studies can have positive and negative impacts for the people concerned. These can range from distress to greater self-understanding for the client/patient; and from feelings of shame about exploiting a client/patient to enhanced learning for the practitioner (Furlong, 2006; Josselson, 1996; Lipton, 1991).

McLeod (2010) provides a comprehensive review of the issues and research relating to the ethics of case studies and discusses the options for best practice. Case study research is a complex undertaking and there are no simple answers. Perhaps the most ethically sound form of case study research is a collaborative process that involves both the client/patient and the practitioner as joint authors, but this may well mean the waiving of anonymity for the client/patient.

Is the method fit for purpose?

There is another aspect to research methods that is worthy of consideration. Is the chosen research method fit for purpose? Again, careful thinking through may reveal some basic flaws in the approach taken. The degree of distance between the researcher and the participant can have ethical implications. It may seem highly appropriate to use a questionnaire or other distance methods as the means of gathering data for large-scale studies. The anonymity and sense of distance may enable some participants to feel more protected. However, there are other aspects that may have ethical consequences. When using non-contact methods the researcher cannot easily monitor the moment-by-moment impact of the research process on the participant. This contrasts with the interview method where a sensitive researcher can respond to the emotional impact of questions appropriately by pausing, checking, slowing the pace, or stopping a particular avenue of enquiry. As well as the emotional impact, such things as the reading and language ability of participants should be considered. This is where a well-conducted pilot study can alert researchers to potential issues. It may be humiliating for a participant to be put in the position of having to admit that they cannot read or understand particular words or use of language. An interview method may enable alternative means of communication to be used.

The ethics of internet and social media research

In recent years, with the dramatic increase in the use of the internet and electronic communication, a whole new area of research methods using social media tools has opened up. A variety of internet and social networking sites are being used by researchers to collect data on a wide range of research areas (see Box 5.5).

BOX 5.5 EXAMPLES OF INTERNET AND SOCIAL MEDIA THAT HAVE BEEN USED IN RESEARCH PROJECTS

Facebook

MySpace

Blogs

Twitter

These sources can give valuable insight into how people represent themselves, live their lives and cope with the daily challenges presented by illness or adversity. Data can be collected across a wide range of geographical areas and from a larger number of people than is possible with other methods. This means that more extensive studies can be undertaken at significantly less cost in terms of time and expenditure (Eastham, 2011).

As well as generating interest and some excitement, these new methods have also raised a number of ethical dilemmas and stimulated debate. Primarily, the dilemmas revolve around the issues of consent, privacy and anonymity. The following types of concern have been expressed. If material is posted on public sites such as blogs or Twitter, is it ethical to use it for research without gaining permission? The material has been posted on these sites by people primarily as a means of communicating with friends, colleagues, relatives and interested members of the public. Although the material is in the public domain, it has not been put there for research purposes. Bruckman et al. (2010) compare this type of research to observational research. They argue that, while observing people in a village square is ethically acceptable, the whole concept of a public space in an online setting is much less clear due to a blurring of the private/public boundaries. This raises questions about whether it is appropriate to seek consent, how consent might be achieved, and whether anonymisation is possible.

It has become clear that, even when attempts to anonymise data have been made, this is fraught with difficulties. In 2008 researchers collected profile data from a cohort of university students and anonymised the data by removing references to the institution, all names and identifying reference numbers. The data was then released for use by approved third parties. The researchers felt that they had anonymised the data adequately and their methods had been submitted to their institutional review board, which granted ethical approval for the study. Within days the anonymity of the university was broken and it was also possible to identify some of the individual students (Zimmer, 2010). The sophistication of search engines is such that given a few descriptive details the risk of the participants being identified is greatly enhanced. Typing perhaps only one sentence into a search engine can reveal a source. Under these kinds of constraints, is it really possible for anonymity be guaranteed?

Researchers have also gained information by 'lurking' on sites, posing as participants in chat rooms and 'friending' people on Facebook. All these methods of gaining access to people with the undisclosed motive of collecting data are ethically questionable. Zimmer (2010) makes a valuable point in urging researchers to foreground the dignity of the people concerned and consider how they might be affected by 'stripping' them of their personal data, without consent, and using it for purposes other than that which they had intended. Internet research is an emergent area but already there is a growing literature on the ethics of the methods. So far it mainly highlights the concerns and dilemmas rather than providing solutions. When making decisions about this type of data collection it is helpful to consider the questions outlined in Box 5.6.

BOX 5.6   THE INTERNET AND CONSENT

Do you need to gain consent from participants if their material is used?

Do you need to gain consent from the site owner(s)?

To what degree is this data public/private?

(Continued)

(Continued)

Is the data readily accessible to the public or is the access restricted in some way, for example, to members of a particular institution, group or site?

Will the means of data collection involve any form of deception (including omission as well as commission)?

Can the data be traced back to an identifiable person?

How can you ensure that individuals are not identified?

Is it possible to provide anonymity for participants and any third parties who may be involved?

A much more detailed set of questions and issues to consider in internet research is to be found in the Association of Internet Researchers' *Ethics Guide* (2012).

Recruitment and participant information: decisions and details

How should people be approached? What are the most ethical ways of conducting recruitment? In the previous chapter we underlined the importance of ensuring that participants are fully informed. How is the initial advertising material best worded to ensure that the participants have maximum choice? How much information should be given and when? There can be a tension between facilitating recruitment and transparency about the research. A thorough and transparent initial flyer may put potential participants off if it seems too complicated and too time-consuming to read. A successful recruitment process usually involves giving complete information about the study but in a staged way. For examples of a flyer and a further information sheet see Boxes 5.7 and 5.8.

BOX 5.7   FLYER EXAMPLE

Research into the experience of first miscarriage

I am a Master's student in counselling at Hightown University and I would like to interview women who have had a first experience of miscarriage in the last two years. I am aiming to gain a detailed understanding of the experiences and needs of women following a first miscarriage so that counsellors will be able to provide more effective therapeutic support.

If you are interested in participating in this research or would like to know more about what it would involve please contact me either by phone on ………. or email ……………..…

An initial flyer giving basic details can be followed by a more detailed email or letter to people who express interest in taking part and an opportunity can be provided to discuss queries.

BOX 5.8 FURTHER INFORMATION FOR PARTICIPANTS

18 May 2013
Dear ...

Research into the experience of first miscarriage

Thank you for expressing interest in participating in this research project. I am a postgraduate student at Hightown University studying for a Master's degree in counselling. I am researching the experience of women who have had a miscarriage for the first time. I would like to interview women who have experienced a first miscarriage within the last two years.

If you agree to take part, the interview will last for one to one-and-a-half hours and can take place at the university or a suitable place of your choice. I will be asking you to tell me in your own words about your experience, including how you felt, what kinds of support you had and what kinds of support you would ideally have liked to have. I will also be very interested to hear about anything else that you feel is important and would like to tell me that is related to your miscarriage. I would like to record the interview and will ask your permission to do this.

You will have the right to stop the interview at any time, refuse to answer any questions if you so wish and I will remove anything from the recording that you would prefer to be deleted at the end of the interview. I will give you details of the local miscarriage support group and the local NHS and private counselling services so that you can contact them if you feel that the research has stirred up any difficult feelings for you.

After the interview I will send you a transcript of the interview for you to read and you will have a further opportunity to remove anything or add anything at this point. Anonymity is guaranteed and all identifying details will be removed from my research dissertation. Anything that you tell me but later do not wish to be included in the research will be kept confidential. You can withdraw from the research at any time up to the end of August 2012 if you feel that you no longer wish to take part and any recordings and transcripts relating to you will be destroyed. When my dissertation is complete I will send you a summary of the findings. You will be able to access the complete dissertation at Hightown University library.

This research project has ethical approval from the Hightown University Research Ethics Committee.

I am a student member of the British Association for Counselling and Psychotherapy and abide by their ethical framework.

My contact details are: mob 01234 56789; email e.manchester@hightown.ac.uk

My research supervisor is Dr George Boston email g.boston@hightown.ac.uk

I will contact you next week to ask if you would like to be interviewed.

Kind regards,
Emily Manchester

Further complete information can then be sent to participants before they have signed a consent form. The consent form should ideally be sent to them to read a week or so before they are asked to sign it to ensure that they are fully aware of what is involved and have time to reflect on their decisions. No immediate decisions relating to participation should be required. For example, it is not acceptable to turn up to an interview and produce a digital recorder and ask at that point if they mind the interview being recorded. Thinking time is needed. Participants can be keen to be helpful but researchers should not take advantage of this generosity. It is important to be alert to and proactive about deference, wanting to please, and lack of understanding in participants. Out of keenness to demonstrate trust or eagerness to get on with the research, participants will sometimes attempt to waive the full ethical and information process. It may feel a bit pedantic at the time but it is important to complete the whole ethical process carefully as researchers can only be sure that they have fully gained consent when this is done. An example of a consent form is given in Box 5.9.

BOX 5.9   AN EXAMPLE OF A CONSENT FORM

Hightown University (official letter heading)

Title of Research Study: The experience of first miscarriage

Researcher: Emily Manchester. Email: emily.manchester@hightown.ac.uk

Research supervisor: George Boston. Email: george.boston@hightown.ac.uk

The participant

I confirm that I have been given detailed information about this study and I have been given the opportunity to ask questions.

I understand that the study will involve an interview and that it will be digitally recorded.

I understand that I can withdraw from this study at any time up to one month before the submission of the research dissertation.

I agree to participate in this study and the data may be used for publication in the researcher's dissertation.

Participant ....   Signature ....   Date ....

The researcher

I undertake to answer any questions that the participant may have about this study.

I will anonymise all identifying references to the participant and any third parties that they may mention.

I will send the participant a transcript of their interview and undertake to remove from the data any material that they do not wish to be included in the study.

I will keep confidential their personal details and any material that they ask to remain confidential.

I will store all the data securely.

If I wish to publish this research more widely, I will request further permission from the participant.

Researcher ....   Signature ....   Date ....

Debriefing and aftercare

Contact with participants does not end with the collection of the data. At the end of the research intervention/process, time should be left for adequate debriefing. The research process may have evoked some difficult feelings for them. Engaging in an experiment, completing a questionnaire, being interviewed may all have after-effects. For some, participation is a highly positive experience and can be beneficial. This good outcome may be due to new insights into how they are thinking about a particular topic; it may lead them to new understandings or evoke a sense that they are not alone or unusual in their feelings and experiences. It may contribute to their own personal and professional development as they may feel stimulated to write or research themselves after having participated in research (Danchev, 2006). Other participants may feel disorientated or disturbed by their participation and require some recovery time. They may have questions to ask. It is also possible that the research will have evoked anxieties or difficult feelings that need to be processed. Providing them with information that enables them to get the support that they may need is an essential part of the process. It is advisable to have pre-prepared information packs relating to the support available in their area that can be given to them either during or at the end of the research contact.

Feedback

Asking the participants how they feel after having participated in the research project and whether the process could have been better in any way provides valuable information for working with future participants and designing new research projects. The participant can be asked for feedback at the end of the research contact in person, by phone or by email. Alternatively, they can be sent a questionnaire. Questionnaires may be individually designed for the particular project or a specially developed questionnaire can be used. The Reactions to Research Participation Questionnaire (RRPQ) in Box 5.10 is a good example of a standard questionnaire that is used in the USA (Newman et al., 2001a).

BOX 5.10   THE REACTIONS TO RESEARCH PARTICIPATION QUESTIONNAIRE REVISED (NEWMAN ET AL., 2001B)

The questionnaire asks for your opinions about what it was like for you to participate in this study. Your responses will be used to help us understand more about what it is like to be a research participant.

I. From the list below, please rank the top three reasons why you decided to partici-pate (1= the most important 2 = second most important, 3= third most important).

___ I was curious   ___ I don't know   ___ I felt I had to
___ To help others   ___ Thought it might improve
                                             my access to health care
___ To help myself   ___ For the money   ___ I didn't want to say no
___ Other (please explain)   _____

II. The following questions deal with your reactions to participating in this study. Please circle the number that best describes your response.

	Strongly disagree	Disagree	Neutral (Maybe)	Agree	Strongly agree
	(No)				(Yes)
1. I gained something positive from participating.	1	2	3	4	5
2. Knowing what I know now, I would participate in this study if given the opportunity.	1	2	3	4	5
3. The research raised emotional issues for me that I had not expected.	1	2	3	4	5
4. I gained insight about my experiences through research participation.	1	2	3	4	5
5. The research made me think about things that I didn't want to think about.	1	2	3	4	5
6. I found the questions too personal.	1	2	3	4	5
7. I found participating in this study personally meaningful.	1	2	3	4	5
8. I believe this study's results will be useful to others.	1	2	3	4	5
9. I trust that my replies will be kept private.	1	2	3	4	5
10. I experienced intense emotions during the research session and/or parts of the study.	1	2	3	4	5
11. I think this research is for a good cause.	1	2	3	4	5
12. I was treated with respect and dignity.	1	2	3	4	5

13. I found participating beneficial to me.	1	2	3	4	5
14. I was glad to be asked to participate.	1	2	3	4	5
15. I like the idea that I contributed to science.	1	2	3	4	5
16. I was emotional during the research session.	1	2	3	4	5
17. I felt that I could stop participating at any time.	1	2	3	4	5
18. I found participating boring.	1	2	3	4	5
19. The study procedures took too long.	1	2	3	4	5
20. Participating in this study was inconvenient for me.	1	2	3	4	5
21. Participation was a choice I freely made.	1	2	3	4	5
22. Had I known in advance what participating would be like I still would have agreed to participate.	1	2	3	4	5
23. I understood the consent form.	1	2	3	4	5

For instructions for scoring see Newman et al. (2001b).

There are also children's and parents' versions of this questionnaire (Kassam-Adams and Newman, 2002).

As well as asking the participants for feedback, it is also essential that the researcher provides feedback for the participants. Ensuring that they are thanked and are told that their contribution is valuable, and explaining what in particular has been useful, are obvious, but sometimes neglected, forms of feedback. If this is not done it can leave the participant with mixed feelings about participating in future research, as Box 5.11 shows.

BOX 5.11   THE ABANDONED PARTICIPANT

I replied to an advert circulated among colleagues by email requesting participants who were experienced counsellors and had worked with clients who raised a particular issue. Jenny contacted me by email, sent some information and we arranged that she would come to my town to interview me a couple of months later. I contacted her a couple of days before the interview as I had heard nothing and wanted to make sure that she was still coming. She arrived on time and I gave her a cup of tea and the interview lasted for about one and a half hours. It felt like a good interview and I found that I had a great deal more to say about my practice in this area than I had previously thought. The interview ended and Jenny went back to her town. A few days later I emailed her. The interview had been recorded and I asked if it was possible for me to have an audio copy or a transcript of it as I wanted to reflect on what I had said. This was for my own personal benefit and not because I wanted to alter the interview in any way. I was happy for all the material to be used. I didn't get a reply and never heard from her again. She had probably had a lot of pressures on her to complete her dissertation, but to never reply even after she had finished her project left me feeling let down and ambivalent about agreeing to participate in future research projects.

This experience underlines that responding to participants' requests, and sending them a letter of thanks with a summary of the research findings completes the process and lets them know that their contribution has been put to good use. Conveying how their participation has led to improvements in processes or practices or that new knowledge and understanding has been revealed by the research demonstrates to them that their time and effort has made a significant difference. It is especially important to give this feedback as there is evidence that a central reason for people agreeing to participate in research is their hope that others may benefit from it (Campbell and Adams, 2009; Ranjbar, 2011).

External safeguards and opportunities for consultation

Voluntary and statutory organisations connected with the research subject area can provide useful ethical guidance. User groups are a particularly valuable source of advice and developing good working relations with them helps researchers to hone their ethical sensitivity in relation to their proposed research.

Throughout the research process the research supervision relationship is probably the most significant factor in helping the researcher to follow an ethical pathway. When the supervisory relationship works well it can be a wonderfully rich and stimulating experience. However, sometimes the supervisory relationship is problematic. Supervisors are often allocated according to their expertise and are not freely chosen. Even if personalities do not fit, the supervisor will usually have a good deal of research experience and expertise, and knowledge of your particular research area. Finding a way of working with them that produces good support for you and your research is well worth the time and effort. Several publications focus on getting the best out of the research supervision relationship and they provide useful reading for novice researchers (Eley and Jennings, 2005; Phillips and Pugh, 2010).

Peer researchers are probably the least anxiety-provoking people to test out your ethical concerns with. They will be having similar struggles. Forming an informal research group can not only provide a source of strong support and advice but also make the process a lot more enjoyable.

Perhaps the most important and emotion-provoking external safeguarding body for researchers is the institutional ethical committee and this is the concern of the next chapter.

REFLECTIVE QUESTIONS

- What aspects of your research are most likely to generate ethical dilemmas?
- Should researchers be able to use material posted on the internet without any restrictions?
- Would you have any concerns if your research data was made available to everyone on the internet?

- What do you think would be the most appropriate way to get feedback from your research participants?
- How can you contribute to establishing a good working relationship with your supervisor?
- What are your views on this information sheet? What would you change/remove/add?

AN INFORMATION SHEET

Hi,

Thank you so much for your interest in my research on significant moments in therapy. I value your contribution to my study and I am writing to highlight the main points in this process:

Research title

An IPA study into significant moments in therapy

Participants

Male or female qualified therapists. These participants need to have experienced what they feel to be significant moments in therapy, and be willing to describe and reflect on their experience by answering a set of open-ended questions.

Research procedure

All participants will take part in a one-to-one, semi-structured interview which will last approximately 1–2 hours. Where and when will be mutually agreed.

Right to withdraw

You will reserve the right to withdraw from participating at any stage of the study.

Ethics

In conducting this research, I am bound by BACP and BASW Ethical Guidelines.

Confidentiality

Confidentiality and anonymity will be maintained at all times. The interview will be transcribed by a third party, bound by confidentiality rules, and you will have the opportunity to proof read, edit and amend this transcript. Names and other personal details will be changed to maintain anonymity. Please note that contents of the transcripts will be discussed with my research supervisor.

(Continued)

(Continued)

Thank you for your time. If you would like to take part in this research or if you have any further questions, please do not hesitate to contact me Victoria@zoomtrack.co.uk

Yours sincerely,
Vicky Edgeburton

References

Association of Internet Researchers (2012). *Ethics Guide*. Accessed on 30 October 2012 at http://aoir.org/reports/ethics2.pdf

Beauchamp, T.L. and Childress, J.F. (2001). *Principles of Biomedical Ethics* (5th edition). New York: Oxford University Press.

Bond, T. (1993). *Standards and Ethics for Counselling in Action*. London: Sage.

Boruch, R.F. (1997). *Randomised Experiments for Planning and Evaluation*. Thousand Oaks, CA: Sage.

Boruch, R.F. (2005). Comments on 'Use of randomisation in the evaluation of development effectiveness'. In G.K. Pitman, O.N. Feinstein and G.K. Ingram (Eds.), *World Bank Series on Evaluation and Development: Vol 7. Evaluating Development Effectiveness*. New Brunswick, NJ: Transaction.

Bruckman, A., Karahalios, K., Kraut, R.E., Poole, E.S., Thomas, J.C. and Yardi, S. (2010). Revisiting research ethics in the Facebook era: challenges in emerging CSCW research. *CSCW 2010*, 6–10 February. Savannah, GA.

Campbell, R. and Adams, A.E. (2009). Why do rape survivors volunteer for face-to-face interviews? A meta-study of victims' reasons for and concerns about research participation. *Journal of Interpersonal Violence*, 24(3): 395–405.

Cooper, M. and McLeod, J. (2010). *Pluralistic Counselling and Psychotherapy*. London: Sage.

Danchev, D.W. (2006). Counselling psychologists' perspectives on professionalism. DPsych thesis, City University, London.

Dubois, J.M. (2008). *Ethics in Mental Health Research*. New York: Oxford University Press.

Eastham, L.A. (2011). Research using blogs for data: public documents or private musings? *Research in Nursing and Health*, 43: 353–361.

Eley, A. and Jennings, R. (2005). *Effective Postgraduate Supervision: Improving the Student–Supervisor Relationship*. Maidenhead: Open University Press.

Flyvbjerg, B. (2006). Five misunderstandings about case study research. *Qualitative Inquiry*, 12(2): 219–245.

Furlong, A. (2006). Further reflections on the impact of clinical writing on patients. *International Journal of Psychoanalysis*, 87(3): 747–768.

Jennings, B., Kahn, J., Mastroianni, A. and Parker, L.S. (2003). *Ethics and Public Health: Model Curriculum*. New Haven, CT: Yale School of Public Health. Accessed on 8 June 2012 at www.asph.org/UserFiles/Introduction.pdf

Josselson, R. (1996). On writing other people's lives: self-analytic reflections of a narrative researcher. In R. Josselson (Ed.), *Ethics and Process in the Narrative Study of Lives* (Vol. 4). Thousand Oaks, CA: Sage.

Kassam-Adams N. and Newman E. (2002). *The Reactions to Research Participation Questionnaires for Children and Parents.* Accessed on 30 July 2012 at www.istss.org/ReactionstoResearchParticipationQuestionnairesforChildrenandParents.htm

Kitchener, K.S. (1984). Intuition, critical evaluation and ethical principles. *The Counseling Psychologist*, 21(3): 43–55.

Lakin, M. (1988). *Ethical Issues in the Psychotherapies.* Oxford: Oxford University Press.

Lipton, E.L. (1991). The analyst's use of clinical data, and other issues of confidentiality. *Journal of the American Psychoanalytic Association*, 39(3): 967–986.

Mark, M.M. and Gamble, C. (2009). Experiments, quasi-experiments, and ethics. In D.M. Mertens and P.E. Ginsberg (Eds.), *The Handbook of Social Research Ethics.* Los Angeles, CA: Sage.

McLeod, J. (2010). *Case Study Research in Counselling and Psychotherapy.* Leicester: British Association for Counselling and Psychotherapy.

Meara, N.M., Schmidt, L.D. and Day, J.D. (1996). Principles and virtues: a foundation for ethical decisions, policies and character. *The Counseling Psychologist*, 24(1): 4–77.

Newman, E., Willard, T., Sinclair, R. and Kaloupek, D. (2001a). Empirically supported ethical research practice: the costs and benefits of research from the participants' view. *Accountability in Research*, 8(4): 309–329.

Newman, E., Willard, T., Sinclair, R. and Kaloupek, D. (2001b). *The Reactions to Research Participation Questionnaire Revised.* Accessed on 11 July 2012 at www.personal.utulsa.edu/~elana-newman/RRPQ-Rforpdf.pdf

Phillips, E.M. and Pugh, D.S. (2010). *How to Get a PhD: A Handbook for Students and their Supervisors.* Buckingham: Open University Press.

Ranjbar, V. (2011). Evidence-based ethical problem solving to guide practice in psychology research. *Europe's Journal of Psychology*, 7(1): 1–7.

Rosenthal, R. (1994). Science and ethics in conducting, analyzing, and reporting psychological research. *Psychological Science*, 5: 127–136.

Salmon, P. (2003). How do we recognise good research? *The Psychologist*, 16(1): 24–27.

Shillito-Clarke, C. (1996). Ethical issues in counselling psychology. In R. Woolfe and W. Dryden (Eds.), *The Handbook of Counselling Psychology.* London: Sage.

Thomasma, D.C., Marshall, P.A. and Kondratowicz, D. (1995). *Clinical Medical Ethics: Cases and Readings: Loyola University of Chicago, Stritch School of Medicine, Medical Humanities Program.* Lanham, MD: University Press of America.

Zimmer, M. (2010). 'But the data is already public': on the ethics of research in Facebook. *Ethics and Information Technology*, 12: 313–325.

6

Research ethics committees: structures and procedures

Research ethics committees (RECs) have come to play a crucial role in research. Most research today needs to obtain specific ethical approval from such a committee before it can begin. Yet this is a recent development and we will consider how this situation has come about before explaining the best way of submitting research to such a committee for ethical approval.

If we turn the clock back to Sigmund Freud's day, his case histories form a cornerstone of his work. One important case study was an eleven-week treatment Freud conducted with a teenage patient called 'Dora'. She was later identified as Ida Bauer and her case was published in 1905 as 'Fragment of an analysis of a case of hysteria'. Freud's portrayal of Dora as a self-obsessed hysterical personality has been widely challenged, and it has been suggested that if Dora were being treated now she would probably be viewed as someone with a borderline personality disorder (Mahony, 1996). While Dora has been a *cause célèbre* for feminist thinkers and psychoanalytic revisionists, there has been a curious absence of ethical reflection about the way in which Freud used the life-story of a teenage patient to underpin his evolving theories, so much so that Dora's life appears to be the psychological stage on which Freud plays the leading role.

We should not be too harsh on Freud, however, as he is merely an illustration of how many people operated, especially in medical and therapeutic contexts, until the 1980s (Aron, 2000). At the very least Freud had thought about the issues, and in his preface to this case he writes:

> I have taken every precaution to prevent my patient from suffering any such injury. I have picked out a person the scenes of whose life were not laid in Vienna but in a remote provincial town, and whose personal circumstances must therefore be practically unknown in Vienna. I have from the very beginning kept the fact of her being under my treatment such a careful secret that only one other physician … can be aware

that the girl was a patient of mine. I have waited for four whole years since the end of the treatment and have postponed publication till hearing that a change has taken place in the patient's life of such a character as allows me to suppose that her own interests in the occurrences and psychological events … have grown faint. Needless to say, I have allowed no name to stand which could put a non-medical reader upon the scent; and the publication of the case in a purely scientific and technical periodical should, further, afford a guarantee against unauthorized readers of this sort. I naturally cannot prevent the patient herself from being pained if her own case history should accidently fall into her hands. But she will learn nothing from it that she does not already know; and she may ask herself who beside her could discover from it that she is the subject of the paper.

(Freud, 1905: 8–9)

This illustrates the ethical dilemma of research with specific people. Freud could not have foreseen, even if he dreamt it, that he would become so influential that his every word would be subject to intense scrutiny. It is clear that he took a range of precautions to protect his patient, yet, in the light of ethical thinking now, we see an absence of: informed consent; confidentiality, extending beyond four years; awareness of patients as potentially vulnerable individuals; and a commitment to the 'other's' well-being, at the expense of scientific advance and knowledge acquisition. While there is an implicit paternalism in Freud's comments, it is clear that he did think ethically to a degree that was far in advance of others at the time. However, in the light of the ease of knowledge acquisition today, particularly through the internet, such a position is untenable today.

As high-profile cases of unethical behaviour have come to light, there has been a growing awareness of the need to ensure the protection of research participants. When people think of examples of ethically controversial research, reference is often made to historic cases. However, it is precisely because there are examples of unethical research still occurring today that the need for, and development of, RECs has been stimulated. RECs take two main forms, which we shall examine, reflecting where research is most likely to be conducted in the UK: the National Health Service (NHS) or through academic institutions. While focusing mainly on these two areas, we will also provide guidance later in this chapter on the ethical application process for research with offenders.

BOX 6.1   THE ACRONYMS USED IN THIS CHAPTER

COREC   Central Office for Research Ethics Committees

DH   Department of Health

ESRC   Economic and Social Research Council

(Continued)

(Continued)	
GMC	General Medical Council
HRA	Health Research Authority
NHS	National Health Service
NOMS	National Offender Management Service
NRES	National Research Ethics Service
REC	Research Ethics Committee

Ethical research and the NHS

Following the Declaration of Helsinki (WMA, 1964), the first form of what we would now call a research ethics committee was established in the UK by the Royal College of Physicians in 1967, focusing on the NHS. Sporadic developments took place until 2001 when the Central Office for Research Ethics Committees (COREC) was established to manage the wide-ranging ethical considerations for the NHS. In 2004 COREC set out standard procedures and instituted an ethical application and approval process that applied equally to individual researchers at degree or postgraduate level and multinational drugs companies. This one-size-fits-all approach was to prove a hindrance to novice researchers and deterred people from engaging in research that needed COREC approval. It also caused ethics to be seen as a bureaucratic process rather than an engagement in the lives of others that enhanced insight, knowledge and relationships.

In its original form the ethical application process was daunting, bureaucratic, slow and inconsistent (Hearnshaw, 2004; Smith, 2004; Wald, 2004). In our experience of such RECs, there was a general bias against qualitative research methods because of their more open-ended nature, often reflecting a lack of experience on the REC itself in these approaches. This has changed as RECs have become more sophisticated in their approaches and more broadly based in their representation (Hedgecoe, 2008), and there are now specific research committees that have been identified or 'flagged' for the receipt of qualitative-based research in the NHS. The development of these specialist committees highlights the issue of complex research applications, which we shall return to later. In 2007 COREC was incorporated into the National Research Ethics Service (NRES) which is now part of the Health Research Authority (HRA) established in 2011. As a consequence the information on the NRES website is being moved across to the HRA website. It is important to understand these developments as previous documents or journal articles will make reference to the form of ethical governance that was in place at the time of publication. For example, Masterton and Shah's helpful article written in 2007 makes reference to COREC, which no longer exists.

In 2011 the Department of Health (DH) issued a document outlining the latest thinking entitled *Governance Arrangements for Research Ethics Committees: A Harmonised*

Edition (DH, 2011) describing what is expected from the National Research Ethics Service (NRES) operated by the Health Research Authority (HRA). Within this structure there are a wide range of RECs. Some have expertise in qualitative research methodologies and others focus on biomedical ethics. RECs are composed of 7–18 voluntary unpaid members, including lay members reflecting public opinion and expert members who have relevant formal qualifications or professional experience. In addition, the 'Research Ethics Service as a whole should reflect the diversity of the adult population of society, taking account of age, disability, gender reassignment, marriage and civil partnership, pregnancy and maternity, race, religion or belief, sex and sexual orientation. This applies to both the lay and expert membership' (DH, 2011: 20). Recruitment is through 'public advertisement in the press, and/or by advertisement via local professional and other networks as most appropriate to the vacancy to be filled' (DH, 2011: 21). Each REC has a chair and deputy-chair to manage the meetings, where minutes are recorded and the confidential discussion of ethical applications for research takes place. Members of a REC are expected to undergo initial training (although the nature of this is not specified) and additional training as required. Each REC can ask for additional expert opinion to be sought.

Ethical research and the universities

In 2005 a major UK research funding body, the Economic and Social Research Council (ESRC), produced its research ethics framework, unifying various individual but fragmented policies that already existed. This marks a development across the whole field of research. ESRC funding is more likely to be found in the university sector and so while there are long-standing RECs in some universities or specific departments in universities, the developments at ESRC and their expectation that their funded research is ethically sound stimulated universities to establish more comprehensive ethical review processes. Many had previously had no ethical review systems in place, as the postgraduate researcher discovered in the example in Box 6.2.

BOX 6.2   CHANGING PATTERNS

When one researcher sought advice about ethical approval for doctoral research in 2006 they contacted the University Research and Commercial Services department at their university. They were given the impression that as they were not doing clinical trials or involving animals why were they bothering this busy department? When they contacted their Faculty they were told the research officer was working on a policy for undergraduates and had not yet developed a policy for postgraduates. Unhappy with these processes, the researcher contacted the Convenor of the Research Committee in their Department and set up an ethical review sub-committee to consider their own and other colleagues' research. This enabled the researcher to state on their participants' information form that the research had obtained ethical approval from a department in the university. The university has subsequently developed a central ethics review process.

Universities in the UK adopt a hierarchical structure for the ethical approval of research. There are two main types of structure. One involves an ethics review process based within the existing structures of departments, faculties, schools or divisions, with a university ethics committee at the highest level. The other involves a separately established ascending series of ethics committees that report to a central ethics committee. The composition of the highest level of university ethical committees varies but is similar to that found in the NHS: approximately ten members drawn from multidisciplinary contexts with a balance of lay representation and ethical expertise.

The main difference is that the latter pattern, and similar to the NHS RECs, uses a centralised application form whereas the first type tend to use locally devised forms until the higher levels are reached. All researchers are required to complete an application form that is submitted for departmental research ethics review, or the first stage of a central ethics committee process, which may be a nominated person or research officer. The purpose is to offer an efficient and quick review process. Many applications do not need to go beyond this review process and are granted approval. As the nature of research and the particular ethical issues it raises vary, if more complex ethical issues are involved it may be necessary for the research proposal to be referred to a higher level. In some instances where there are significant ethical issues, the research will be forwarded to the central university ethics committee. If further guidance or consideration is required, applications are forwarded through the ethical review hierarchy until final approval for the research to go ahead is given or final rejection is received.

The existence and extent of university research ethics review processes reveals the seriousness with which the ethical obligations for research are taken. However, as we shall see later in this chapter, at times this is driven by a desire to protect the institution rather than by an intellectual and philosophical commitment to the well-being of others.

As part of good research practice, universities offer guidelines on conducting ethical research for the reason that indemnity or insurance cover would be invalid if the research had not been granted ethical approval. This can cause dilemmas for students on time-limited courses: if ethical approval is delayed there is a great temptation to recruit participants using sub-optimal criteria, out of the anxiety of not finding sufficient participants. Yet to do so can place the researcher and the university at risk.

The benefits of ethical governance and research

While there have always been some examples of good practice relating to research ethics in institutions, the *laissez-faire* approach to research ethics of the last century has become formalised into structured systems. The aim is to prevent harm to participants and in order for the institutions concerned to protect themselves. Information about ethical governance commonly contains statements that place a high value on knowledge, expertise and integrity. Researchers are expected to demonstrate the ability to conduct research to high standards of scholarship and ethics. Universities and NHS Trusts want to show that they are responsible institutions that can be trusted.

Given these developments, what are the intended functions of RECs, university RECs or similar bodies performing the same function?

First, a function of RECs is to promote ethically approved research for the well-being and health of others. The intention is not to set up bureaucratic structures that inhibit research. Many use standardised application forms, which, despite their cumbersome nature, enable equity of practice and a common framework with which members of RECs can become familiar. They are helpful for identifying simple mistakes, such as failing to include an example of an information sheet for a particular piece of research.

Secondly, there is a clear intent by ethics committees to protect the individual. All such organisational processes arose out of concerns about the unethical medical and psychological research that was conducted on research participants without their consent or understanding of any risks that might be involved. Like many other areas in society at large, the increase in litigation seeking legal redress and financial compensation has been the driving force in regulation and compliance. A previous generation of researchers may not have realised the power dynamic and imbalance inherent in many research contexts. RECs offer a proactive and protective approach that has well-being for the other at its heart. That protection applies to the researcher as well.

Thirdly, researchers can be encouraged to adopt the view that ethical approval is a validation of the thought they have given to their research, successfully passing the scrutiny of other interested researchers on the REC. A REC can offer ethical guidance at the application stage in order to minimise risk and help the researcher. For example, researchers can negotiate not to maintain confidentiality, but to use named sources on the basis of ethical transparency and, most importantly, the preference of the participants. Attention paid by a researcher to these areas adds clarity to the research that aids its passage through the ethical approval process.

Fourthly, the existence of a REC could be seen as a resource to be used creatively. This is the function of those teaching ethics in research contexts. They can present ethical compliance as a useful development that produces well-thought-through projects, rather than as a burden to be endured. Some university research committees are proactive in putting forward this positive aspect of their role and contribute positively by running training sessions for applicants, writing case studies demonstrating good ethical practice, and offering workshops for potential researchers.

The limitations of ethical governance and research

Any system of governance that tries to balance multiple and at times conflicting needs and demands with ethical issues is always going to have its limitations. It is helpful to know what these might be in advance as part of the preparation for this process.

First, a frequently made critique is that RECs protect the institution rather than the individual. By adopting a utilitarian focus, such RECs reduce ethics to a formulaic, instrumental position and fail to develop other forms of ethical frameworks rooted in community, co-operation and shared governance (Christians, 2011). This is reflected in the traditional composition of such committees, which draw on people who adopt a bio-medical model of persons and advocate quantitative approaches. There is a fear that the genuine pursuit of knowledge and the intellectual curiosity essential to good research will be limited by the bureaucratic procedures and controls adopted by RECs (Tierney and Corwin, 2007). Inflexible adherence to controls at times limits the scope of research, as is shown by the example in Box 6.3.

BOX 6.3   RECS CAUTIOUS AND CONFORMING

Helen wanted to examine the experience of children and young people (aged under 18) whose parent or parents had been a drug user. She wanted to explore how this had shaped the children and young people and their subsequent psychological development.

There are very few pieces of qualitative research with this age group as they are hard to recruit. Helen made contact with a charity that supported such young people and gained ethical approval for this research from their managing committee. Helen's re-search was undertaken for a Master's degree and it also required ethical approval from her university. On the basis of Gillick competency (Hunter and Pierscionek, 2007) and the fact that the interviews would take place with a project worker also present in the room, Helen was optimistic that ethical approval would be given.

The university ethics committee made it conditional that her research could only go ahead with the written approval of the parent or parents. On one hand, this fits with standard expectations (Angell et al., 2010; Brierley and Larcher, 2010). However, it failed to take into account the complexity of family situations where young people were often part of one, two, or three reconstituted families. It overlooked the professionalism of the organisation the young people were attached to and their own wish to participate in the research (Newman et al., 2012). It failed to think realistically about the needs of the researcher as the Master's programme required the thesis to be completed within nine months. It also failed to think about what would be reasonable in practice given the minimal level of risk involved. It devalued the young people's right to describe their own experience. This research could potentially bring new insights and new voices to a rarely heard group. While the researcher could have appealed, making her case at the next tier of ethical review, this would have delayed her data collection and threatened the successful completion of her research within a fixed time frame.

Secondly, there is a clear imbalance of power. The ethical admonition to do no harm has resulted in Australian, British and North American ethical committees becoming 'increasingly powerful, intrusive, demanding and insatiable, such that ethics is now restricted and stymied in ways scarcely credible a few decades ago' (Scott, 2008: 18–19). Scott's research is related to the sexual abuse of children and there is a concern that much-needed research will fail to receive ethical approval or will only proceed in a 'watered down' form. Lichtman (2011) surveys the North American scene and comes to a similar conclusion.

Thirdly, there is a perceived bias against qualitative or non-traditional methodologies. This has been researchers' experience both in the USA and the UK (Lichtman, 2011; Richardson and McMullan, 2007). While the NHS has recognised this and adapted its structures to be more representative, a colleague experienced what he perceived as a 'grilling' at an NHS REC when he was challenged about the open-ended nature of his interview questions on the basis they were potentially harmful. A statement was made: 'Wouldn't a questionnaire be less intrusive?' He was examining how parents coped with the death of a child and the value of chaplaincy support services. He had put in place a link to an independent member of the hospital staff who could offer support through the use of counselling and listening skills. Details were also provided for help-lines and local voluntary bereavement groups. He explained that very often such parents feel that their voice gets lost in a medical setting and they wanted to tell their story so that it could be of benefit to others. Such an outcome would not have been as clear or as powerful if limited to a questionnaire. He also pointed out that the sample size of the proposed research group was far too small for acceptable statistical validity if a questionnaire were used. While ethical approval was given, the interaction betrayed the limited understanding or biased perceptions about some research methods.

Fourthly, while a great deal of time and effort is put into research approval, much less is done in terms of monitoring whether approved research is conducted ethically. RECs can do little about dubious or unethical actions such as plagiarism, misrepresentation, deceit and falsifying data. It is unclear how this could be done without RECs becoming even more power-laden and adopting a 'policing' role (Richardson and McMullan, 2007). In the view of many, this would be a detrimental step (Denzin and Lincoln, 2011).

Fifthly, a critique from the USA is that ethical research and governance arises out of an implicit Anglo-Saxon culture that fails to be sufficiently flexible to address issues of cultural difference. Canella and Lincoln (2011) identify studies from Italian and Mexican settings in the USA that challenge implicit assumptions about the nature of health, well-being and confidentiality. This is an ongoing bias that needs to be addressed in the UK. Issues of cultural and ethnic difference need to be considered not at a surface level, but in terms of a critical examination of the underlying philosophies that form European and Western culture.

Sixthly, a complex question to answer, but one that must be raised, is 'Who defines risk?' While researchers are often asked in applications to identify any risks, there is a failure to define what such a risk might be. In an earlier example, a NHS REC wanted to limit the scope of the research questions so as to avoid potential harm to the participants. This committee had an implicit understanding of risk and were adopting a risk-averse approach. Yet the researcher demonstrated that there is always a risk in any research but that careful steps had been taken to minimise it in the first place and deal with it if it arose subsequently. Institutions tend to be risk-averse and some see ethical review committees as increasingly problematic in this area (Zywicki, 2007).

A step-by-step guide for submission to a research ethics committee

It can be very daunting when starting out on research to be faced with a complex online process and detailed but confusing websites that are full of acronyms. So we will now cover the steps that apply to all the processes. The university and NHS systems are then described in more detail and guidance is provided for applications for research with offenders.

The following steps apply in all research contexts, and will aid preparation for gaining ethics approval (see Box 6.4).

BOX 6.4   INITIAL STEPS FOR ETHICS APPLICATIONS

1   Read existing ethical codes or frameworks.
2   Identify whether the research is an audit or service evaluation.
3   Write a research proposal.
4   Obtain and complete the forms.

---

1. Make yourself familiar with the ethical codes or frameworks that exist in your research area. For example, as such documents are often influenced by changing legislation (available at www.esrc.ac.uk/about-esrc/information/research-ethics.aspx), the ESRC research ethics framework (mentioned above) is continually being revised and so it is important to access the latest version. Such frameworks make explicit the ethical principles that underpin such research and identify the commitments of any researcher.

2. Identify if your research is dealing with previously collected anonymised data or is classed as an audit. What is viewed as an audit varies from place to place so it is best to check if in doubt. Some researchers have confessed they have tried to avoid an ethical review process by calling their research an audit, not because what they were trying to do was intrinsically unethical, but simply to avoid the bureaucracy involved (Richardson and McMullan, 2007). The National Research Ethics Service (NRES) has published a document which helps to clarify the difference between research, clinical audit, service evaluation and usual practice/surveillance work in public health (it is available at www. nresnhs.uk/applications/is-your-project-research/ and another version can be found at www.nres.nhs.uk/applications/guidance/research-guidance/?entryid62ethical66984). Audits normally use existing data and are conducted internally to the institution or organisation. So where a researcher is looking at how to improve existing services, the results are not applied to other external contexts and are not for dissemination beyond the service involved, this is generally viewed as an audit. Audits do not normally require ethical approval, but there are always borderline cases where research participants are interviewed and these may require appropriate ethical approval even if the overall project is termed an audit. It is also crucially important to note that if we take responsibility to the 'other' seriously and are engaging in a relational ethics process, we still have an ethical obligation even if formal ethical review and approval is not required. The Royal College of Psychiatrists has developed helpful advice for ensuring high ethical standards in relation to clinical audits (see www.rcpsych.ac.uk/crtu/centreforqualityimprovement/ ethicalaudit.aspx, accessed on 8 December 2012).

3. Most research projects have a number of constituent parts requiring critical consideration that are likely to be scrutinised by a REC. Write a draft research proposal and

submit this to any internal ethical review processes that exist. If no formal processes exist, researchers could evolve a peer-review process with other colleagues or trainees. This could enhance not only the quality of ethical reflection but also the quality of the overall research project. This begins with the clarity of the research question. Most new researchers find it difficult to focus their interests down to a very specific area, however the broader the research the greater the likelihood of an increased number of ethical concerns. It is helpful to adopt a title that contains a specific research question and an introduction outlining what motivation lies behind the research. This leads to an appropriately focused literature review that underlines and supports the need for this particular research. At this point a consideration of research methodology, showing an awareness of the philosophical issues around knowledge, truth and meaning, leads into a rationale for the chosen research methodology and a detailed description of the method, including a discussion of ethical considerations. RECs pay specific attention to the design of the research, the rationale for the chosen methodology, and the method, especially how participants will be recruited (for example, number, age, gender, exclusion/inclusion criteria). A REC is likely to contain more researchers from a quantitative background simply because this research tradition has been doing more research for a longer period of time. This is not to set up a false dichotomy between qualitative and quantitative research; both are essential for generating knowledge and insight for theory and practice (Brannen, 2005). Yet some REC members, because of their research background, will be more questioning about the forms of recruitment used in small qualitative studies, such as 'snowballing' (Noy, 2008), which is helpful in accessing hidden or hard-to-reach groups (Rubin and Babbie, 2009). Having collected appropriate data, how this is analysed is also of importance to RECs. If using quantitative methods, attention needs to be paid to suitable forms of statistical analysis. If using qualitative methods, there needs to be clarity about how the textual ideas are representative of the participants, showing the link between what the person says and how this is understood by the researcher.

4. In each research project there are practical steps that are vital for the successful ethical approval process and good quality research. Participant information sheets are very important and require care in writing in order to combine a readable style that allows participants to acquire sufficient clarity about the research without it reading like a legal document. This is best tested before submission on someone who is not involved in the research but who is able to give direct and honest feedback. Consent forms are also essential and need to be written in a way that fits with the ongoing process of informed consent. It would be helpful for the REC to know that this is sent in advance of the research, allowing sufficient time for the research participant to absorb the information and ask questions. This guards against any unconscious coercion of participants and demonstrates a relational ethic of care. Any REC will also want clarity about confidentiality and data protection. This could include a definition of what confidentiality is, identifying who has access to the research material, and ensuring compliance with data protection, including the suitable storage and/or deletion of material after the research is complete. These important steps are summarised in the checklist in Box 6.5.

BOX 6.5 INFORMATION REQUIRED FOR A RESEARCH PROPOSAL

Title

An introduction outlining the motivation behind the chosen research project

A focused literature review that indicates the need for the research

The research question(s) and aims

A description and justification of chosen methodology

The method and process of data collection, including recruitment and how quality, validity and reliability are to be ensured

Ethical considerations and researcher reflexivity

How the data will be analysed and discussed

How the results will be disseminated

An estimate of the time and financial costs involved

References

Appendices, which may include the following:

- Example of advertisement/flyer for recruitment
- Participants' information sheet
- Agreement to participate and permission forms (e.g., to digitally record data)
- Letters requesting and confirming ethical permission, etc.
- Copy of proposed interview questions/questionnaire or other data collection information
- Post-interview information for participants (including sources of support and/or a resource pack)

You are now in a position to make a formal submission to the appropriate REC. Having obtained the correct form or online document, complete all sections as required. Where it is unclear, check on the online support available, read any FAQs or contact the appropriate research person attached to the review process. Incomplete forms or missed questions can result in significant delays in obtaining ethical approval. Start this process as soon as is feasible. All such applications take time and any delay in ethical approval puts a researcher under pressure in time-limited circumstances. It can be important to find out when RECs meet and how regularly, so you can plan to apply at the best time. The dates for the NHS RECs are available online.

Applying for university ethics approval

Universities often provide a checklist to aid the completion of the ethics application form. If no checklist exists in your academic institution, Iphofen (2011) has produced a helpful generic ethical review checklist aimed at social research but applicable in wider contexts. Guidance on the ethical review process is normally found in course handbooks or from course tutors or programme leaders. The illustration in Box 6.6 shows the kinds of experiences that postgraduates have when submitting applications for university ethics approval.

BOX 6.6   TWO UNIVERSITY ETHICS APPLICATIONS

Two trainee researchers made their ethics application at the same time to the same committee. Amy was doing a qualitative study interviewing staff about their lived experience of delivering certain psychological interventions on the basis of a week's in-service training. Her ethical approval was returned quickly. May was also doing a qualitative study, interviewing parents about their lived experience of the psychological support they had received because their child or children had long-term and sometimes terminal health conditions. These interviews were to be conducted in the home of the parents. The ethical committee asked May to review her application and clarify her rationale for interviewing at home and what steps she had put in place for her own safety. May had not thought about this at all in her original application. In her response, May identified the steps she would take for her safety: she would have a definite time for the appointment that was known by others; she agreed that she would ring a colleague when the interview was finished; she would ask a colleague to ring her if she had not rung them within 30 minutes of the end of the stated interview time. The committee also wanted to know what support she could offer the parents if the interview subject generated distress. May responded that she would offer information about sources of confidential support. The committee were happy with these additional steps and granted ethical approval.

As is evident from the example in Box 6.6, the safety of researchers and their participants is an important factor in the decisions of ethical committees. In the example in Box 6.7 the researcher had not covered this aspect at all.

BOX 6.7   RESEARCHER AND PARTICIPANT SAFETY

One university ethics committee dealt with complex non-medical ethical issues raised by the research studies of students and staff. One case referred to it related to a doctoral researcher who wanted to examine the marginalisation of women in society, focusing

(Continued)

(Continued)

on prostitutes/street workers. There were immense ethical difficulties the researcher had not thought about, most notably the risk to herself and her participants, which, it was felt, betrayed a lack of genuine understanding about the subject. It was a real possibility that the street workers might be harmed if their pimps realised that they were talking to an outsider. While it was agreed this was an important area to research and that this group were under-researched, the conclusion was reached that the risk to the researcher and the risks to street workers outweighed the potential benefits of such research and so ethical approval was not given for this particular study.

Recent experience with a university REC resulted in four applications being returned. One had missing information as several questions had been overlooked. Another had not attached a participant's information sheet. A third had not indicated the possible questions to be asked in the semi-structured interview method they had adopted. The fourth raised concerns about young people aged 16 being interviewed without parental consent. The first three were dealt with quickly and the delay was less than two weeks. The fourth required some major rethinking of strategy by the researcher and delayed the project by six weeks. This unsettled the researcher, who took longer to get into their work as a consequence.

Each university will have a common set of ethical expectations but some may have additional criteria. These are usually soundly based but occasionally the additional criteria can present the researcher with unexpected ethical issues. For example, an American university with a strongly religious background has as one of its ethical guidelines concerns about research proposals which involve any element that goes against the ethos of the institution. If that university were to take a particular stance on homosexuality, one wonders how it might deal with a research proposal to explore the psychological benefits of gay marriage?

Applying for NHS ethics approval

The application for NHS ethics approval in the UK is a longer and more complicated process, often involving the researcher being asked to attend the REC. This process is outlined in the Application Process Flowchart (available at www.nres.nhs.uk/).

The researcher applies to the NRES (HRA) for ethical approval for research in the NHS using the online integrated research application system if the research includes past or present users of services provided by the NHS and participants identified because of their status as relatives or carers of past or present users of NHS services. It is easy to fall into the trap of thinking that ethical approval from a REC is needed for everything involved with the NHS, but this not always the case and it is important to identify this at an early stage. For example, a research project limited to questionnaires or interviews with staff or managers would no longer require review by a REC. While ethical approval from a REC was formally required for research involving NHS staff recruited as research participants by virtue of their professional role, this was changed and is no longer required from September 2011. However, if this research is being conducted under the auspices of a university, ethical approval is still required through their research ethics committee structures. In October 2010 one trainee therapist on placement in a NHS psychotherapy service wished to examine the lived experience of being a psychotherapist in the NHS in a specific service. She was told that she could not do this without NHS ethical approval through a REC. She was not able to do this in the time available and so her research focused on other therapists in the voluntary sector. If she had been doing this in October 2011, she would not have needed REC approval, but would have been able to the use the central university research ethics committee. In an NHS context requiring attendance at the REC, it is important to pre-pare thoroughly. Consider the kinds of questions that you could be asked and prepare concise responses.

Research with offenders

The application process to do research with offenders, either in prison or on pro-bation, requires the same ethical considerations as those expected for the National Research Ethics Service. If the research is focused on the healthcare of offenders, an NRES application is required first, with additional permission sought through the National Offenders Management Service (NOMS). If the research is focused on offenders, then direct application to NOMS is the best option. An extract from the Ministry of Justice's website explains how to apply to do research through the National Offenders Management Service:

> All applications to conduct research across NOMS (prison and probation) must be made using the standardised NOMS research application form … or through the Integrated Research Application System IRAS – the latter also enables applications to be made to various health and social care bodies. The NOMS approval process extends to research in Young Offenders' Institutions (YOIs), but excludes research in Secure Training Centres, Secure Children's Homes or with Youth Offending Teams – applications to conduct research in these areas should be directed to the Youth Justice Board.
>
> When submitting an application form to NOMS, the guidance within AI 02/2012 must be followed. Applications should be fully completed and the appropriate supporting docu-mentation should be provided – the form should be accompanied by applicant CVs, any ethical submissions and approvals, and any questionnaires, consent forms etc that have already been devised. Incomplete applications are likely to delay the review process. All research applications will be reviewed against the following criteria:

1   Are there sufficient links to NOMS' priorities?
2   What are the anticipated demands on resources (e.g. anticipated demands on staff time, office requirements, demands on data providers)?

3   Is there an overlap with other current/recent research?
4   How appropriate and robust is the methodology to be applied?
5   Are there any data protection/security issues?
6   Are there any ethical considerations?
7   What is the extent of the applicants' research skills and experience?
    (National Offender Management Service, 2013)

The steps we have outlined in various chapters throughout this book should enable you to complete criteria 6. What is being looked for is the application of general ethical principles to the prison or offending contexts, so an additional degree of thought is required by the researcher. The example of obtaining informed consent from prisoners, given in Chapter 2 (Box 2.5), highlights many of the issues that need to be addressed. As the ethical processes are more complex in these settings, it is important to leave a longer period of time for this stage of the research process to be completed.

Revisions

If the ethics committee requires revisions to the research project, attend to these quickly rather than seeing it as an impossible setback for the entire project. Initially requests for revisions can evoke strong emotions, such as anger or feelings of failure, however it is important to hold in mind that these revisions will probably enhance the research.

Conclusion

Pauwels (2007: 8) writes:

> The Ethics Review process resembles the small child in Hans Christian Andersen's fairytale 'The Emperor's New Clothes'. It is about getting to the heart of the matter, avoiding the human susceptibility to be easily deceived and challenging predispositions to social conformity. Ethics is about telling the truth and it is central to scientific integrity.

Ethics review processes have made a significant contribution to safeguarding the welfare of participants and ensuring that positive benefits are gained from research. Research ethics committees are relatively new ventures and many are still undergoing development. Where ethical review has become overly bureaucratised, formulaic and defensive under the guise of protection, we can find ourselves in an uncomfortable dialogue with research ethics governance.

We started this chapter with a reference to Freud's clinical case, Dora. Freud became famous and historians of psychoanalysis have revealed Dora's identity. One could argue that revisionists of Freud have used the actual naming of Dora as a means of developing their critique of him, rather than thinking about what might be the outcome for Dora and her descendants. Here is an ethical dilemma. Is it for the greater good that Freud's ideas are questioned or challenged, even though the process of doing so means exposing someone from whom consent could not be gained? Or does our commitment to the participant, in this case Dora, limit a critique of Freud that relies on revealing her identity? There is no straightforward answer to this. While Freud may be an exceptional case, it is also clear that research participants belong to a family and a community and that needs to be borne in mind.

In conclusion, we have explored why RECs (in various forms) exist, what their functions are, what their limitations are and how this contributes to a broad-based discussion of research ethics review. In addition, we have outlined how researchers can find their way through ethical approval processes. This is all so that vital research can take place in a way that balances the needs of the institution and the researcher with a genuine care of the 'other'.

REFLECTIVE QUESTIONS

- Are there colleagues that you can talk to who have already been through a similar ethics process?
- What are the strengths of your proposed research and what benefits will it offer?
- Are there areas of your ethics application that might be considered controversial?
- How might you use your existing professional experience to support your proposal?
- Can you defend your methodology?
- What preparations do you need to make in order to face a group of up to 15 people asking you challenging questions about your research?

References

Angell, E., Biggs, H., Gahleitner, F. and Dixon-Woods, M. (2010). What do research ethics committees say about applications to conduct research involving children? *Archives of Disease in Childhood*, 95: 915–917.

Aron, L. (2000). Ethical considerations in the writing of psychoanalytic case studies. *Psychoanalytic Dialogues*, 10(2): 231–245.

Brannen, J. (2005). Mixing methods: the entry of qualitative and quantitative approaches into the research process. *International Journal of Social Research Methodology*, 8(3): 173–184.

Brierley, J. and Larcher, V. (2010). Lest we forget… research ethics in children: perhaps onerous, yet absolutely necessary. *Archives of Disease in Childhood*, 95: 863–866.

Cannella, G. and Lincoln, Y. (2011). Ethics, research regulations, and critical social science. In N. Denzin and Y. Lincoln (Eds.), *Sage Handbook of Qualitative Research* (4th edition). Thousand Oaks, CA: Sage.

Christians, C.G. (2011). Ethics and politics in qualitative research. In N. Denzin and Y. Lincoln (Eds.), *Sage Handbook of Qualitative Research* (4th edition). Thousand Oaks, CA: Sage.

Denzin, N. and Lincoln, Y. (Eds.) (2011). *Sage Handbook of Qualitative Research* (4th edition).Thousand Oaks, CA: Sage.

Department of Health (2011). *Governance Arrangements for Research Ethics Committees: A Harmonised Edition.* London: Department of Health. Accessed on 1 December 2012 at www.dh.gov.uk/prod_consum_dh/groups/dh_digitalassets/@dh/@en/documents/digitalasset/dh_133993.pdf

Freud, S. (1905). Fragment of an analysis of a case of hysteria. *Standard Edition of the Complete Psychological Works of Sigmund Freud* (Vol. 7). London: Hogarth Press.

Hearnshaw, H. (2004). Comparison of requirements of research ethics committees in eleven European countries for a non-invasive, interventional study. *British Medical Journal,* 328: 140–141.

Hedgecoe, A. (2008). Research ethics review and the sociological research relationship. *Sociology,* 42(5): 873–886.

Hunter, D. and Pierscionek, B.K. (2007). Children, Gillick competency and consent for involvement in research. *Journal of Medical Ethics,* 33: 659–662.

Iphofen, R. (2011). *Ethical Decision-making in Social Research: A Practical Guide.* Basingstoke: Palgrave Macmillan.

Lichtman, M. (Ed.) (2011). *Understanding and Evaluating Qualitative Educational Research.* Thousand Oaks, CA: Sage.

Mahony, P. (1996). *Freud's Dora: A Historical, Textual and Psychoanalytic Study.* New Haven, CT: Yale University Press.

Masterton, G. and Shah, P. (2007). How to approach a research ethics committee. *Advances in Psychiatric Treatment,* 12: 220–227.

National Offender Management Service (2013). National Offender Management Service website. Accessed on 6 March 2013 at www.justice.gov.uk/publications/research-and-analysis/noms

Newman, J., Van't Hoff, W., Callens, C., Tibbins, C. and Davies, H. (2012). What do young people want? Information requirements on clinical research. *Archives of Disease in Childhood,* 97: A79.

Noy, C. (2008). Sampling knowledge: the hermeneutics of snowball sampling in qualitative research. *International Journal of Social Research Methodology,* 11(4): 327–344.

Pauwels, E. (2007). *Ethics for Researchers: Facilitating Research Excellence in FP7.* Luxembourg: Office for Official Publications of the European Communities. Accessed on 14 April 2013 at www.ec.europa.eu/research/.../Ethics/Useful.../ethics-for-researchers_en.pdf.

Richardson, S. and McMullan, M. (2007). Research ethics in the UK: what can sociology learn from health? *Sociology,* 41(6): 1115–1132.

Rubin, A. and Babbie, E. (2009). *Essential Research Methods for Social Workers* (2nd edition). Belmont, CA: Brooks/Cole.

Scott, C. (2008). Ethics committees and research. In H. Piper and I. Stronach (Eds.), *Don't Touch: The Educational Story of a Panic.* Abingdon: Routledge.

Smith, R. (2004). My last choice. *British Medical Journal*, 329.

Tierney, W. and Corwin, Z. (2007). The tensions between academic freedom and institutional review boards. *Qualitative Inquiry*, 13(3): 388–398.

Wald, D. (2004). Bureaucracy of ethics applications. *British Medical Journal*, 332: 282–285.

World Medical Association. (1964). Code of Ethics of the World Medical Association: Declaration of Helsinki. Helsinki, Finland: WMA June 1964. *British Medical Journal*, 2: 177.

Zywicki, T. (2007). Institutional review boards as academic bureaucracies: an economic and experiential analysis. *North Western University Law Review*, 101(2): 861–896.

7

The social and political contexts of research and the ethics of dissemination

Solyom (2004) argues that research in medicine is of itself a social good. This is equally true for counselling, nursing and social work research. It aims to benefit society by throwing light on previously unexplored issues and improve practice. This chapter explores the need for researchers to sensitise themselves to the social and political impacts of their work. We also consider the responsibilities that continue to exist after a research project has been completed. The need to close the ethical research cycle by ensuring that research findings are disseminated appropriately is emphasised and the ethical dilemmas that can arise in relation to dissemination are discussed. The wider level of ethical responsibility, to make any significant new understandings known to social policy makers, the media and the general public, is highlighted and debated. Finally, we consider the context of research and the ethical implications of obtaining research funding and researching within organisations.

Practitioners in counselling, social work and nursing are registered or accredited by professional and statutory bodies and regarded as professionals by the general public. We are sanctioned by the society within which we practice. Through our work we are profoundly connected to the social world and cannot confine our practice to individual work (Tjeltveit, 1999). Because our work is intimately connected to the social world, the political dimensions of our endeavours as practitioners should not be ignored. This is as true for research as for all the other aspects of our work.

Social workers often have a well-developed sense of the social and political impact of their work but, accustomed to the bounds of confidentiality and individual work, people from other branches of the caring professions can be wary of becoming engaged at societal and political levels. This is perhaps especially true for counsellors and psychotherapists, who are deeply immersed in individual work and can feel a sense of separation from the social and political world. However, even apparently highly individual dealings with clients and patients have an external impact.

Politics acts at a micro-level as well as at a macro-level and it can be argued that through operating from an ethical basis in their daily professional lives practitioners are engaging in political acts. How we deal with clients and patients has an impact that is wider than the one-to-one relationship. This perspective is supported by Peperzak, Critchley and Bernasconi (1996), who cite Levinas's view that ethics and politics are inextricably linked through the relationship with the other: 'The order of the state rests upon the irreducible ethical responsibility of the face-to-face relationship' (Peperzak et al., 1996: 161). The Hobbesian view is that peace in society is maintained by opposition to the threat of war (Peperzak et al., 1996). Levinas, in contrast, underlines the importance of peace and proximity. If we treat others responsibly, with sensitivity and respect, this has an impact on them and it encourages them to behave more ethically in their turn towards others. In this way the one-to-one ethical relationship creates an outward ripple that impacts on the social and political context.

Acting with kindness, thoughtfulness and compassion towards others and taking responsibility for our actions in our daily work and when we engage in research can, of itself, engender positive change. Aristotle's original vision for ethics was that it would not just benefit the individual, but was primarily for the benefit of the *polis* – the wider community. It is important to view ourselves and our participants as part of wider systems. This links with Levinas's view of the other as being situated within the full context of their humanity. Recognising this means that we need to embrace the social, political and ecological implications of our world of work.

Bystanding

In their interactions with participants the researcher also takes the position of a witness and this carries with it added responsibility. Whatever form of research is undertaken, the researcher's act of witnessing involves receiving information about participants' lives that may not have been disclosed to others. Sometimes it will involve highly sensitive data and moving narratives. Once we have received these details or heard these stories there is the additional task of ensuring that we are faithful to participants in the use of the material they have provided. Rather than just being a passive receptor, something more active is called for. While this usually concerns getting the most out of the data and disseminating the results within the bounds of our agreement with participants, sometimes a form of social injustice may become clear to us. The question to consider here is does the researcher have an obligation to do something about it?

Becoming aware of injustice and remaining passive in relation to it can evoke feelings of powerlessness and guilt. It places the researcher in the position of a bystander to another person's suffering. Researchers may not have chosen to be in this position, but hearing about such an issue elicits a feeling of pressure to find a way of acting to lessen the injustice. Clarkson (1996) argues that the right course of action in this situation involves moving from the passive position of bystander to that of active witnessing and 'standing by'. It follows that an awareness of social responsibility is an integral part of the research encounter and it should encompass the social, cultural and ecological contexts of the research.

Individual researchers may not feel that they have the capacity to become activists themselves, but someone may be able to derive some good from their findings. Anderson (2009) recognises that at times researchers may feel that their actions are unlikely to contribute to achieving social change, but she reminds us of Gandhi's saying: 'Almost everything that you do will seem insignificant, but it is very important that you do it.' In many situations the right form of action will be to publicise the research findings without compromising participants' anonymity and bring any forms of injustice to the notice of funders, policy makers and relevant activist groups. Occasionally, more focused individual action than publicising research is required. As previously mentioned in Chapter 2, if a participant discloses something that involves serious and immediate harm to themselves or a third party, there is a need to take direct action. It is important to flag this up in the initial research information so that participants are aware of what might happen when researching areas where this situation might occur.

Social and political involvement

It is apparent that although the political implications of their research may have not become clear to them at the outset, the process of engaging in their study has led some researchers to become more deeply involved. Following their experience of interacting with participants, they have felt motivated to become involved with an action group, a support group or voluntary organisation.

Research for social change

So far we have looked at issues that need wider action that has become clear during the research process. However, research can be undertaken with the primary aim of attaining social change and researchers themselves may have personal histories and experience of activism that they may wish to put at the service of their clients and patients (Anderson, 2009; Bemak, 2009).

The recognition that research may be a powerful means of achieving social change has been gathering momentum at least since the work of Marx and Engels in the nineteenth century. Marx made the powerful statement that 'the philosophers have only interpreted the world, the point is to change it' (Marx, 1845). In the 1960s, with increasing focus on empowerment and emancipation, movements began to emerge that acknowledged the potential power of research in transforming participants' lives. It was increasingly recognised that all research proceeds from a particular perspective or view of the world, and that the standpoint of the researcher needs to be identified. It was also becoming clear that research outcomes are influenced by the context in which the research takes place. Organisations, institutions and governments commission research that is framed from particular viewpoints. For example, medical settings may implicitly frame the research in terms of the medical model. This happened with early disability research, which was approached from a perspective of deficit.

[Disability research] … until the 1990s … rarely involved disabled people in the research process. … Moreover, as most of it was founded on individual medical or deficit explanations of disability, it also served to reaffirm traditional negative assumptions about disabled people and the causes of disablement.

(Barnes, 2009: 459)

The history of disability research highlights the fact that if researchers lack awareness of the political contexts of their research, they can cause harm by simply reproducing the status quo.

Transformatory research

To attempt to redress these distortions and achieve greater social justice for participants a variety of forms of enquiry were developed, such as participatory research, action research, co-operative enquiry research, and emancipatory research. These developments were inspired by the works of Freire (1970), Fanon (1961) and Gramsci (1971) and their view that research should be undertaken with the primary aim of achieving social and political change. Researchers choose and design their research area with a social and political impact in mind and with the purpose of attaining significant change in relation to a particular issue. Research that includes aspirations for change at a social and political level is regarded as transformatory (Dona, 2007).

Feminists (Cahill, 2004), disability activists (Barnes, 2003; Zarb, 1992), refugee workers (Dona, 2007) and community psychologists (Nelson and Prilleltensky, 2010), among others, have been significant contributors to the development of research approaches that are transformative in nature. Their methodologies highlight the hidden mechanisms of everyday power relations described by Foucault as 'the microphysics of power' that maintain injustices and discriminatory practices (Foucault, 1977: 26). Lincoln (2009) makes the point that power and power relations almost always underlie ethical issues in research. This creates a need for researchers to develop the ability to deconstruct the frameworks that support the power relations that are to be found in all aspects of research, from individual relations to the institutional, social and political contexts within which it is taking place.

These approaches have not been without their critics. Some researchers feel that engendering social change is outside their remit or capacity. Others have highlighted the need for care in that such research could stimulate protest among participants and this could then attract the attention of powerful authorities who subject them to further forms of oppression. A further criticism is that politically committed researchers simply produce the results that they set out to find (Silverman, 1998). This view is firmly rebutted by Barnes (2009), who argues that if the researcher is transparent about their standpoint and the research process, and ensures that their methods are rigorous and open to scrutiny, then readers can make an informed judgement about the value of the research.

A key factor in producing ethically sound transformative research is the maintenance of reflexivity and openness to being wrong in the face of strongly held views. In fact it has been argued that reflexivity and activism are closely linked. Kobayashi asserts that 'an activist stance follows both logically and morally from a self-reflexive one' (Kobayashi, 2003: 346). If you are able critically to examine your underlying motivations and consider the perspectives of others, then you are more likely to be able to identify restrictive contexts and the need for change. It is also evident that engaging in such research can involve challenges for the researcher as they may be called upon to recognise their own role in oppressive practices.

Transformative research encompasses a variety of methods but key elements are the inclusion of participants and their organisations throughout the research process. This is not to be undertaken in a tokenistic way but involves considerable effort to ensure and enhance the agency of participants and achieve equity in power between researchers and participants. It includes sharing control over the nature and accessibility of the research produced. The overall aims are to facilitate the voices of the disempowered, to highlight injustice and to deconstruct socially pervasive, negative perspectives in relation to marginalised people. The role of the researcher is to facilitate the research rather than to act as a leader.

As well as enabling the lives and circumstances of people to be revealed, it has also been recognised that the research process itself can be transformatory for participants. Cahill, a participatory action researcher, in recognising the fluid nature of subjectivity, underlines that the research process has a significant impact on participants and they 'shift and create new identities for themselves' (Cahill, 2007: 270). She researched a project entitled 'Makes me mad: stereotypes of young urban womyn of colour' with six young women in New York City. The co-researchers led the research and were involved throughout the process, including identifying questions, the overall design, the analysis and the dissemination of findings (Cahill, 2004). Through telling and analysing their stories of discrimination and repression, the women not only gained new perspectives on the issues that they faced, but also developed an entirely new view of themselves. Cahill (2007) links this process to Freire's concept of *conscientização*, which can be translated as 'consciousness raising'. Freire (1970) argues that the oppressed internalise negative images of themselves and it is only by facilitating their awareness of the contradictions in their social and political circumstances that they can become aware of the means of their oppression and move towards change. The oppressed, Freire says, are the unheard. Therefore enabling them to break the silence of their situation by telling their stories and to experience being heard forms an important part of this process.

Another important facet of these forms of research is the sharing of data with all the individuals and groups involved. In this way, it is possible for everyone to understand more deeply the positions of all the contributors and this underpins future democratic decision-making processes (Lincoln, 2009). Lincoln highlights the importance of authenticity in research. She advocates five forms of authenticity, and two types are especially important here. The first is that there should be an element of catalytic authenticity to the research. Some aspect of the research needs to have the potential to reveal something new about the issue being researched: 'questions should be of compelling interest, as well as holding promise of some beneficence for stakeholders' (Lincoln, 2009: 154). She also underlines the need for tactical authenticity. This means that, having completed the research, it may be necessary to ensure that participants and co-researchers have the ability to take their new knowledge forward. This may involve training in public speaking or ensuring that support or action groups are formed.

Must all research be transformatory?

While it is admirable that research can contribute to social change, novice researchers should not feel that their research has to do this. If student research can throw light on new areas, then this is excellent, but undergraduate and Master's level postgraduate study is aimed primarily at familiarising students with research methodologies, methods and processes. The task is to design and carry out a research project. So is it enough to argue that achieving a qualification by itself is an adequate reason for embarking on research and taking participants' time? The answer to this is yes if it means that another research-minded practitioner will be out in the world with the ability to critique and utilise research appropriately to make the best possible interventions with clients and patients. Additionally, rather than seeking new practice knowledge, it may be that research is undertaken to advance particular research methods or produce research instruments or tools. Research need not always be emancipatory or transformatory, but researchers do need to develop an awareness of the social and political influences on their work.

End of the research process or another beginning?

When a research project has been completed, this is not the end of ethical engagement with the research. Dissemination is the next process that has ethical implications. Dilemmas about how to promote research findings sensitively and effectively abound. Dissemination derives from the Latin verb *disseminare*, to scatter seeds. At best, this is exactly what should happen to research. Findings ideally should generate more ideas within the academic and practice communities, stimulate new ways of thinking for practitioners, generate new studies, and contribute to positive changes and developments.

How can the knowledge that has been gained be best used? Closing the research circle by disseminating the findings is the obvious option, but how far this should extend requires active consideration. Who needs to know? Sometimes the answer will be a very wide audience and best practice is to try to get the research published in the ways that will ensure that the findings get the greatest possible airing.

When we think about research dissemination, first thoughts tend to be in the direction of writing academic papers for the benefit of other academics, practitioners and researchers, and disseminating results to participants. When considering who needs to know, we should cast our net widely and produce our research results in a variety of formats so that it is accessible to the widest range of people. It is especially important that accessible means are found to communicate with people who experience a diverse range of disability. The criterion to keep in mind is that it will be clear and easily understood. Academics and professionals can tend to become so immersed in specialised language that they lose awareness of the fact that they are excluding everyone except specialists in their fields. Research findings can be communicated to almost any audience if enough thought and creativity is put into the task. Results can be represented in a variety of formats and media, including drama and the visual arts, and the range of dissemination could extend from peer-reviewed journals to articles in the general press, interviews and the diverse forms of social media.

At other times more restricted dissemination is necessary. The greatest ethical dilemmas arise around restriction. For example, findings from one study that show that a particular application of therapy is less efficacious than another is important for practitioners and researchers in the field. A wider circulation may result in negative press headlines ('Therapy does not work!') or be taken up out of context by politicians who wish to restrict health and social funding. Sometimes the personal nature of the research findings means that dissemination has to take a different form (see Box 7.1).

BOX 7.1   AN ALTERNATIVE WAY OF GETTING THE IMPORTANT MESSAGES OUT

Zelma gathered information on the lives of people living in a refuge and the services provided for them. She was faced with an ethical dilemma that lay between needing to protect the identity of the participants and her agreement with the refuge managers who wanted her to publish the research because they wanted to challenge the stereotypical views of the people who came to refuges and the daily life in the refuge. Zelma felt that she could not use the participants' stories but came up with a creative alternative. She agreed to run a series of workshops for allied professionals based on the recommendations from her research and aimed at challenging stereotypes.

As Waterman (1988) points out, the scientific method can provide us with relevant facts … but it cannot tell us which ends are good; and science cannot tell us what is right or obligatory. To answer questions about goodness and rightness, we must rely on ethics.

(Tjeltveit, 2000: 246)

Of course it can be argued that the findings of thorough research should be disseminated even if there are to be negative consequences. Perhaps the answer is to ensure that research is disseminated responsibly and, the most important point, in its context. Emphasising the context of research is crucial if distortions of its findings are to be avoided. In Box 7.2, Christian Jarrett draws our attention to a student dissertation that was highlighted out of context and then misattributed in the academic press.

BOX 7.2   HOW THE MISREPORTING OF A STUDENT DISSERTATION WRECKED BEREAVEMENT COUNSELLING'S REPUTATION

It has become the received wisdom in psychological circles that bereavement counselling is at best ineffective and at worst harmful, especially when offered to people experiencing 'normal' grief. Why the dire reputation? According to counselling psychologists Dale Larson and William Hoyt [2007], it's thanks largely to inappropriate reporting of an unpublished student dissertation by Barry Fortner, in which it was claimed 38 per cent of bereaved clients would have fared better if, instead of receiving counselling, they had been in the no-treatment control group.

The trouble, Larson and Hoyt argue, is that Fortner's 1999 dissertation has only been cited once, by his colleague Robert Neimeyer in 2000. Since then, over 14 studies have reported the 38 per cent figure, but each time they have cited Neimeyer's published paper (a summary of past research), not Fortner, thus giving the misleading impression that the result came from a piece of quality, peer-reviewed empirical research.

Worse still, like a game of Chinese Whispers (or Telephone, if you're American), recent papers discussing the 38 per cent figure have cited not only Neimeyer, but also subsequent papers citing Neimeyer, thus giving the impression that the 38 per cent figure has been corroborated by later investigations!

But now Larson and Hoyt [2007] have hit back. In a journal article and technical analysis (the latter is freely available online), they claim that Fortner's methodology, which led to the 38 per cent figure, is flawed. Moreover, they asked the American Psychological Association Publisher Gary VandenBos to submit Fortner's dissertation to a *post hoc* peer review. And according to Larson and Hoyt, 'The experts conclusively agreed that [Fortner's methodology] is seriously flawed and that there is no valid basis for the claim that 38 per cent of grief counselling clients suffered deterioration' [Larson and Hoyt, 2007: 352].

Apart from Fortner's 38 per cent statistic, the reputation of bereavement counselling has also suffered from the reported outcomes of three key meta-analyses (where the outcome data from lots of studies is lumped together), one of which is in Fortner's dissertation.

For example, the most extensive of the meta-analyses, published by Allumbaugh and Hoyt in 1999, is often reported as having found poor efficacy for bereavement counselling. But according to Larson and Hoyt [2007], the efficacy rates in the 35 assessed studies varied hugely, due mainly to differences in whether clients had referred themselves and how long they had been bereaved. If the analysis was confined to the recently bereaved, and to those who had chosen to receive counselling, then compared to [the] no-treatment control [group], counselling showed the kind of benefits typically found for other types of psychological therapy for other conditions.

Larson and Hoyt acknowledge the need for more research and conclude: '...findings to date indicate that cautious optimism, rather than the recently fashionable dire pessimism, is the attitude most congruent with empirical findings on grief counselling outcomes' [2007: 354]

Source: Christian Jarrett (2007) *BPS* [British Psychological Society] *Research Digest*. Reproduced with permission.

First steps in dissemination for new researchers

For the new researcher, dissemination can seem a daunting prospect. Perhaps it is best approached in stages. Presenting research findings to fellow students or work colleagues can be a good way to start. It provides an opportunity to practise summarising research findings, answering questions and is often a valuable source of feedback. This can be followed by summarising the research findings on a poster to be displayed in the poster section at a conference. Many professional conferences have sessions allocated for the presentation of student research. This typically involves a 20-minute presentation followed by 10 minutes of questions. Engaging in these forms of dissemination can help researchers to hone the presentation of their research findings and move towards preparing them for publication.

Journals and papers

When considering writing a paper for a journal or professional publication, the first step is to review the range of possible outlets. Look carefully at how the papers in these publications are written in terms of both content and style, and read the advice given to prospective contributors. Then choose the ones that seem to be most in tune with the completed research. It has to be acknowledged that some journals favour particular forms of research and writing styles. It can feel frustrating to know that if the research study is represented in the style that seems most faithful to the work, it is possible that this will reduce the likelihood of its publication. The importance of giving your results a wider airing has to be weighed against the restrictive feeling of not being able to write in your preferred style. This is especially relevant for qualitative researchers, who may have to condense their findings so much as to cause anxiety about losing the degree of complexity that it is important to represent. To remain faithful to the detail of participants' experiences it may be best to think about writing several papers – each about an aspect of the research – rather than trying to convey the overall findings in one paper.

It can be helpful to send a preliminary email to a prospective journal asking the editor if they would be interested in a paper on the subject of your research. The process of submitting a paper usually involves peer review by two or three reviewers after the paper is submitted. Each reviewer will give an opinion and the editor will reply to the author with a decision to reject the paper, resubmit it with revisions or to accept it as it is. If it gets rejected, try not to lose heart. If the work is controversial or on the cusp of a paradigm change, then extra effort may be needed to get it published. Rejection happens to even the most revered academics. Developing the stamina to persist and the ability to read reviewers' comments constructively is essential. Sometimes it takes several versions and submission to a number of journals before it is published. Bear in mind that successful people are usually those who have the ability to deal with setbacks constructively. It can be argued that persevering in the endeavour to get research results disseminated is an important part of the ethical responsibilities of researchers. It is also worth noting that the process of review and reply can sometimes take a long time. It is worth contacting the editor if you have not heard to ask where your paper is in the process. One researcher fortunately had the courage to follow-up a gap in communication about his paper (see Box 7.3).

BOX 7.3   THE MISLAID PAPER

George sent a paper to a journal editor. He was really pleased to hear that it had been positively reviewed and the editor said that it would be published in the journal. A year later he had heard nothing further and was getting increasingly worried about it as he was about to start applying for academic jobs. He knew that his publication record was a really important part of his CV and could be a pivotal factor in whether he was successful. On enquiring, he discovered that the editorship of the journal had changed and in the hand-over his paper and the reviews relating to it had been mislaid. If he hadn't chased it up, his paper might have lain undiscovered in a pile on someone's desk and would never have been published.

While thinking about the publication of research, we cannot resist adding a plea for transparency of method when writing for journals. Reading research papers in journals is sometimes a surreal experience for seasoned researchers. The research process is often depicted as a straightforward, uncomplicated process, as if it proceeded in an immaculate fashion. But an entirely smooth process is unusual. Perhaps research would move forward at a faster pace if transparency of method also included more rigorous transparency about process. Being transparent about setbacks helps other researchers to avoid mistakes. It also helps novice researchers to understand that setbacks are an integral part of the research process and not necessarily due to their inadequacies.

There is a further layer of ethical concern about publishing papers in commercial journals. Recently, controversy has arisen about this form of dissemination. It was brought sharply into focus when The Wellcome Trust found that it could not access a paper on research that it had funded without paying a fee. UK universities currently pay the publishers of journals around £200 million a year for access to research that is largely publicly funded (Jha, 2012). The Wellcome Trust, which takes the view that research is not completed until it is published, now requires that the research that it funds is made available to everyone via open access publishing. They also highlight problems with the selection of papers for publication because they feel that commercial journal editors lack the required level of research expertise and their need to make a profit can lead editors to select research for publication because of its potential to generate media interest rather than for its scientific value (The Wellcome Trust, 2012).

Wider media

There are often aspects of research findings that would interest and benefit the general public and a much wider form of dissemination is called for. This could involve researchers appearing on radio or TV or contributing to newspaper and magazine articles. However, it is also important to be aware that it is not unusual for published research to be misused by people wanting to make a particular point. Researchers therefore have an ethical responsibility to monitor how their research is being used. Some newspapers are prone to misrepresent research with a frequency that raises a good deal of concern.

This issue has been the subject of submissions to the Leveson Inquiry into the conduct of the press (Association of Medical Research Charities, Cancer Research UK and The Wellcome Trust, 2012). While there are newspapers that report research responsibly, more than a few distort findings so regularly that it can only be concluded that their motivation has more to do with selling their product than accurately reporting the work of researchers. At times it involves a simple misunderstanding resulting from confusion about the meanings of correlation and causality. Researchers should be aware that on some newspapers the journalists writing about research are not specialists and they can have very short deadlines. It is not usual for them to check their stories with the researchers concerned and sometimes the distortions are extreme, as Sumner et al. (2011) found when details of their research were released coincidentally at the time of the 2011 urban riots in the UK (see Box 7.4).

BOX 7.4   RIOT CONTROL: HOW CAN WE STOP NEWSPAPERS DISTORTING SCIENCE?

Our team recently made an interesting discovery: that in a certain part of the brain, the concentration of a neurotransmitter called GABA – which regulates signalling between neurons – is related to a certain type of impulsive personality. More specifically, we found that people who had lower levels of GABA in a part of their frontal lobe also reported higher 'rash impulsivity'. People who score higher on rash impulsivity tend to act more rashly in response to strong emotions or urges. Our results tallied with recent genetic findings that linked GABA to alcoholism and drug abuse: disorders in which high rash impulsivity is a common feature. We wrote up our study for publication in a scientific journal and, as standard, we were encouraged by our university to issue a press release.

As the riots unfolded, news stories based on our research began appearing. On Tuesday 9 August, a newswire story by the Press Association announced that 'Brain chemical lack "spurs rioting"', with 'spurs rioting' printed mischievously in quote marks, falsely implying these were our words. In a further creative leap, *The Sun* heralded a 'Nose spray to stop drunks and brawls', and that a 'cure could be developed in the next ten years'. *The Sun* has since retracted its article following a complaint from us, although the original text of the article can still be found.

The Daily Mail asserted that 'Rioters have "lower levels" of brain chemical that keeps impulsive behaviour under control', and repeated these false assertions in the caption of a subsequent opinion piece: 'Do rioters, pictured looting a shop in Hackney, have lower levels of a brain chemical that helps keep behaviour under control? Scientists think so'. Before long these dangerous claims had been repeated across many news outlets and blogs in the UK and worldwide (on Thursday 11 August 2011 a Google search for 'Riot',

'GABA' and 'Dr Frederic Boy' produced 25 stories, including articles from India, Russia and Malaysia, and pieces in Polish and Finnish).

Source: Sumner, P., Boy, F. and Chambers, C. (2011). Riot control: how can we stop newspapers distorting science? *The Guardian* [online], 22 August. Accessed on 10 August 2012 at www.guardian.co.uk/science/blog/2011/aug/22/riot-control-newspapers-distorting-science. Reproduced with permisson.

There are several points in the pathway to the general public where distortions of research may occur. Universities and organisations are often keen to publicise excellent research and send out press releases. Researchers need to check press releases to ensure that the publicity material is accurate and does not talk up research findings or present them out of context. Once the findings are out in the public domain they are much more difficult to control.

The next level is the media. Researchers need to keep an eye on how their research is being represented. Any misuse needs to be highlighted and action taken. Chambers and his team, who were involved in the example quoted above, insisted that their complaint was heard by the Press Complaints Commission. It takes time and energy to achieve redress, but if research is to be more responsibly reported then this has to be seen as part of the research process. One can only imagine the distress that has resulted from press misreporting in areas such as cancer research where positive developments in treatments are represented as 'cures'.

How can the researcher guard against misrepresentation? A first step is to consider the ways in which the findings might be distorted or misrepresented. Then, when engaging with press officers or journalists, take care to give a balanced view and ask about the context in which the research might be used. Consider producing summaries of different levels of complexity to cater for a range of audiences. In information summaries, Chambers (2012) recommends including sections entitled 'What this study shows' and 'What this study does not show'. Be aware that journalists sometimes attend conferences and report on what they hear there. Take advantage of any media training that your institution or employer may provide. If journalists make contact, do not be bounced into giving them an immediate response. Take the time that is needed to think through the implications of what is being asked. If misrepresentation occurs, point out the problem and ask for a retraction to be printed. If a good response is not forthcoming, complain to the relevant media body. Finally, remember that there is the option to refuse to engage with the media or answer particular questions.

Dissemination via the internet

There are increasing numbers of researchers who are publishing their research on the internet. This is a tremendous advancement, enabling access to research for any interested party. This positive move has to be balanced with care as the research is likely to reach a very wide international audience. Clarity of communication, use of language and contextual information are especially important to ensure that misunderstandings do not arise.

Using the creative arts

Keen and Todres (2007) urge researchers to be more creative in the dissemination of their research. They are especially keen that research findings are used to improve understanding and practice. This is, they say, often viewed as beyond the remit of researchers. In a review of research dissemination, they highlight researchers who have utilised the arts effectively to communicate their findings.

'Handle with Care' is an example of research-based theatre about the experiences of women with metastatic breast cancer (Gray, 2000). It was performed over 200 times in Canada and the USA. On evaluation, it was found to be beneficial to service users, family members and health professionals alike. Similarly successful dramatic productions have addressed the impact of prostate cancer on the lives of men and their families (Gray et al., 2003), and the experience of psychosis (Mienczakowski, 2003). Knowles and Cole (2008) describe many other examples in the expanding field of the use of creative arts in research methods and dissemination.

The meaning of dissemination for participants

When gaining written consent from participants, as well as stating that the research will be used for an academic qualification, it is often usual practice to add 'and any publications' to the final line on the forms to cover all dissemination eventualities. But is this really fair to participants and does it constitute informed consent? This is especially pertinent in relation to qualitative research where participant stories may be involved. Even if the participants were fully aware that their data would be published in an academic paper, did the researcher or the participants realise that this could be taken up by the press? How might participants feel if they saw their stories published in the popular press? And is it possible that they could be identified by a third party? How might it affect their organisations or the public perception of their situation? All this needs a good deal of forethought. It also indicates that sound ethical practice probably involves gaining specific permission for each form of publication as the need arises. Perhaps the more just position to operate from, when considering dissemination, is to think in terms of joint ownership of the data. The research data is best regarded not as the exclusive property of the researcher or the research sponsors, but shared between all the parties involved.

Dissemination by participants and their organisations

In mainstream research it is taken for granted that researchers have the right to represent participants in the dissemination of the research. Researchers from the participatory field often involve their participants, their co-researchers, and the communities who have taken part in their projects in the dissemination process. These methods enable participants to represent themselves in the way that they feel most accurately and appropriately represent their concerns (Manzo and Brightbill, 2007).

Events using the creative arts have proved to be an especially successful means of communicating research findings and recommendations (Cieri and McCauley, 2007; Tolia-Kelly, 2007). However, participant dissemination has its own ethical considerations. Manzo and Brightbill (2007) highlight several aspects that present added dilemmas. Where findings are likely to be controversial or increase the vulnerability of participants, dissemination decisions need to be timely and carefully measured against the harms and benefits that may ensue. In particular, anonymity is unlikely to be maintained and in some social and political circumstances making participants' concerns and strategies explicit can lead to further oppression. Politicising ordinary people through participation in a research project could place them in positions of vulnerability that they would otherwise have avoided. At best, participation and shared power involves the deepest degree of respect for participants; at worst, it can take on the appearance of a confidence trick, masking manipulation and the imposition of a researcher's or another group's interests or worldview.

Funders

In considering the social and political contexts of research it is also important to reflect on the implications and ethics of receiving funding for projects. In universities, academics are under mounting pressure to obtain research grants. Allied to this, universities are increasingly forming partnerships with commercial organisations. There is also a movement of research out of universities. We do not have the statistics for the UK, but it is interesting to note that, in relation to medical research in the USA, in 1994 63 per cent of clinical trials were taking place in universities. Today this number has shrunk to 26 per cent (Lemmens, 2008: 748). Lemmens (2008) warns that corporate contributions to academic research are increasing and expresses concern that the independent and critical academic sector is diminishing. Barnes (2003) has raised concerns about the encroachment of market forces into organisations and institutions involved in the production of research, and the increasing financial insecurity of many researchers who are on short-term contracts. All these forms of pressure, subtle though they may be at times, can influence decisions and impact on sound ethical practice.

At the outset of a project a researcher may be in the privileged position of receiving funding. Funding can take a variety of forms, such as equipment, conference funds and salaries. However, it is also necessary to consider the ethical implications of accepting financial support. Is this funding entirely neutral or is there an agenda underlying the commissioning of the research? Some important points to clarify are who will own the research and will its dissemination be controlled? And what would happen if the research produced findings that would impact negatively on the funders? Has it been agreed that the research can be published even if there is a negative outcome for them? The *British Medical Journal* has become so concerned about the withholding and misreporting of data from clinical trials relating to drugs in current use that it now requires all relevant anonymised, patient-level data to be made available (Godlee, 2012).

It is evident that there are aspects of funding that need to be thought through. Care taken in drawing up any contracts with funders at the outset of the research project can ensure that biases are avoided or minimised. Finally, if research is funded, this information must be included in any publications so that readers can fully understand the research context.

Conclusion

In this chapter we have emphasised the need to gain and maintain an awareness of the social and political contexts of research. Our view is that it is not possible to operate ethically as a researcher in an asocial and apolitical bubble. Facing the issues that arise in these arenas can be anxiety-provoking and it takes courage to speak openly about concerns. The first inkling that there is something that needs to be addressed is usually a feeling of discomfort and dissonance. Further examination of the feeling with the help of a colleague or supervisor may be necessary to clarify the issue concerned. Meeting the challenge has the valuable reward of peace of mind.

We have also underlined the importance of completing the research process by finding a means of disseminating the research findings in a way that ensures that new knowledge gets to the people who need to know about it and also respects the privacy and safety of participants. A commitment to transparency and responsibility is contained within effective dissemination. Mindfulness of the welfare of participants, as always, has to be at the centre of the process. In the first chapter we drew attention to the commitment to vocation that is evident in people who work in the caring professions. As Lemmens (2008) says, if researchers stay connected to a sense of a higher calling, this will enable them to sustain an ethical approach to research.

REFLECTIVE QUESTIONS

- What are the social and political dimensions of your research project?
- Are there any external pressures that might influence the direction of your research?
- Do you feel that it is important that research stimulates some form of social or political change?
- What do you think would be the most appropriate means of disseminating your research?
- If your research gained media attention, how might this impact on you, your participants, or any third parties (including organisations) that may be involved?
- Who will own your research?

References

Allumbaugh, D.L. and Hoyt, W.T. (1999). Effectiveness of grief counselling: a meta-analysis. *Journal of Counselling Psychology*, 46(3): 370–380.

Anderson, A. (2009). On being an activist. *Journal for Social Action in Counselling and Psychology*, 2(1): 44–50.

Association of Medical Research Charities, Cancer Research UK and The Wellcome Trust (2012). *Leveson Inquiry: Culture, Ethics and Practice of the Press*. Accessed on 1 December 2012 at www.wellcome.ac.uk/stellent/groups/corporatesite/@policy_communications/documents/web_document/wtvM054159.pdf

Barnes, C. (2003). What a difference a decade makes: reflections on doing 'emancipatory' disability research. *Disability and Society*, 18(1): 3–17.

Barnes, C. (2009). An ethical agenda in disability research: rhetoric or reality? In D.M. Mertens and P.E. Ginsberg (Eds.), *The Handbook of Social Research Ethics*. London: Sage.

Bemak, F. (2009). The roots of social justice: the personal journey of a human rights activist. *Journal for Social Action in Counselling and Psychology*, 2(1): 51–56.

Cahill, C. (2004). Defying gravity? Raising consciousness through collective research. *Children's Geographies*, 2(2): 273–286.

Cahill, C. (2007). The personal is the political: developing new subjectivities through participatory action research. *Gender, Place and Culture: A Journal of Feminist Geography*, 14(3): 267–292.

Chambers, C. (2012). Scientists and journalists need different things from science: discuss. The Royal Institution public lecture, 13 March.

Cieri, M. and McCauley, R. (2007). Participatory theatre. In S.L. Kindon, R. Pain and M. Kesby (Eds.), *Connecting People, Participation and Place: Participatory Action Research Approaches and Methods*. Abingdon: Routledge.

Clarkson, P. (1996). *The Bystander*. London: Whurr.

Dona, G. (2007). The microphysics of participation in refugee research. *Journal of Refugee Studies*, 20(2): 210–229.

Fanon, F. (1961). *The Wretched of the Earth*. New York: Grove Weidenfeld.

Foucault, M. (1977). *Discipline and Punishment: The Birth of the Prison*. New York: Vintage Books.

Freire, P.R.N. (1970). *The Pedagogy of the Oppressed*. New York: Herder and Herder.

Godlee, F. (2012). Clinical trial data for all drugs in current use. *British Medical Journal*, 345: 7.

Gramsci, A. (1971). *Selections from the Prison Notebooks*. London: Lawrence and Wishart.

Gray, R. (2000). Graduate school never prepared me for this: reflections on the challenges of research-based theatre. *Reflective Practice*, 1(3): 377–390.

Gray, R., Fitch, M., Phillips, C., Labrecque, M. and Greenberg, M. (2003). Managing the impact of illness: the experiences of men with prostate cancer and their spouses. *Journal of Cancer Education*, 18(4): 223–229.

Jarrett, C. (2007). How a student dissertation destroyed bereavement counselling's reputation. *BPS* [British Psychological Society] *Research Digest*. Accessed on 21 November 2012 at http://bps-research-digest.blogspot.co.uk/2007/08/how-student-dissertation-destroyed.html

Jha, A. (2012). Wellcome Trust joins academic spring to open up science. *The Guardian* [online], 9 April. Accessed on 18 November 2012 at www.guardian.co.uk/science/2012/apr/09/wellcome-trust-academic-spring

Keen, S. and Todres, L. (2007). Strategies for disseminating qualitative research findings: three exemplars. *Forum: Qualitative Social Research*, 8(3): 17.

Knowles, G.J. and Cole, A.L. (Eds.) (2008). *Handbook of the Arts in Qualitative Research.* Thousand Oaks, CA: Sage.

Kobayashi, A. (2003). GPC ten years on: is self-reflexivity enough? *Gender, Place and Culture: A Journal of Feminist Geography*, 10(4): 345–349.

Larson, D.G. and Hoyt, W.T. (2007). What has become of grief counselling? An evaluation of the empirical foundations of the new pessimism. *Professional Psychology: Research and Practice*, 38: 347–355.

Lemmens, T. (2008). Conflict of interest in medical research: historical developments. In E.J. Emanuel, C. Grady, R.A. Crouch, R.K. Lie, F.G. Miller and D. Wendler (Eds.), *The Oxford Textbook of Clinical Research Ethics*. Oxford: Oxford University Press.

Lincoln, Y.S. (2009). Ethical practices in qualitative research. In D.M. Mertens and P.E. Ginsberg (Eds.), *The Handbook of Social Research Ethics*. Los Angeles, CA: Sage.

Manzo, L. and Brightbill, N. (2007). Towards a participatory ethics. In S.L. Kindon, R. Pain and M. Kesby (Eds.), *Connecting People, Participation and Place: Participatory Action Research Approaches and Methods*. Abingdon: Routledge.

Marx, K. (1845). Thesis 11. Thesen uber Feuerbach. In K. Marx, *Marx-Engelswerke*, band 3. Berlin: Dietz Verlag. Accessed on 5 December 2012 at www.mlwerke.de/me/me03/me03_005.htm

Mienczakowski, J. (2003). The theatre of ethnography: the reconstruction of ethnography theatre with emancipatory potential. In N. Denzin and Y. Lincoln (Eds.), *Turning Points in Qualitative Research: Tying Knots in a Handkerchief*. Palo Alto, CA: AltaMira Press.

Nelson, G. and Prilleltensky, I. (Eds.) (2010). *Community Psychology: In Pursuit of Liberation and Well-being* (2nd edition). Basingstoke: Palgrave Macmillan.

Peperzak, A.T., Critchley, S. and Bernasconi, R. (Eds.) (1996). *Emmanuel Levinas: Basic Philosophical Writings*. Bloomington, IN: Indiana University Press.

Silverman, D. (1998). Research and theory. In C. Seale (Ed.), *Researching Society and Culture*. London: Sage.

Solyom, A.E. (2004). Ethical challenges to the integrity of physicians: financial conflicts of interest in clinical research. *Accountability in Research*, 11: 119–139.

Sumner, P., Boy, F. and Chambers, C. (2011). Riot control: how can we stop newspapers distorting science? *The Guardian* [online], 22 August. Accessed on 10 August 2012 at www.guardian.co.uk/science/blog/2011/aug/22/riot-control-newspapers-distorting-science

Tjeltveit, A.C. (1999). *Ethics and Values in Psychotherapy*. London: Routledge.

Tjeltveit, A.C. (2000). There's more to ethics than codes of professional ethics: social ethics, theoretical ethics, and managed care. *The Counseling Psychologist*, 28(2): 242–252.

Tolia-Kelly, D.P. (2007). Capturing spatial vocabularies on a collaborative visual methodology with Melanie Carvalho and South Asian women in London. In S.L. Kindon, R. Pain and M. Kesby (Eds.), *Connecting People, Participation and Place: Participatory Action Research Approaches and Methods*. Abingdon: Routledge.

Waterman, A.S. (1988). On the uses of psychological theory and research in the process of ethical enquiry. *Psychological Bulletin*, 103: 283–298.

The Wellcome Trust (2012). *Open Access Journal Frequently Asked Questions*. Accessed on 12 November 2012 at www.wellcome.ac.uk/About-us/Policy/Spotlight-issues/ Open-access/Journal/WTVM051948.htm.

Zarb, G. (1992). On the road to Damascus: first steps towards changing the relations of disability research production. *Disability, Handicap and Society*, 7(2): 125–138.

Index